What people are say:

WhatsApps from Heaven

An inspiring and comforting book... it's beautiful!
Theresa Cheung, author of *The Truth about Angels*

WhatsApps from Heaven astonished me. It gave me chills. An incredible must-read for those enduring grief and for those who are looking for signs from beyond.
G.L. Davies, author of *Haunted: Horror of Haverfordwest*

A moving love story... This is not the first time I have heard of messages from the deceased that use new electronic gadgets. This is indeed a development which should be expected because the communication from the next level of life has followed the means available in our dimension to communicate with us.
Anabela Cardoso, author of *Electronic Contact with the Dead: What do the Voices Tell Us?*

Three categories of evidence collectively prove that life continues after bodily death: scientific, clinical and experiential. Louise shares her comforting and inspiring signs from Patrick that convince her life and love do not die... Kudos, Louise, for having the courage and love to share your wonderful experiences.
Mark Pitstick MA, DC, director of *SoulPhone Foundation*, founder of *Greater Reality Living Groups*

A fascinating first-hand account of the importance of anomalous phenomena surrounding personal loss, and how continued spiritual bonds can benefit our health and well-being.
Dr Callum E. Cooper, editor and author of *Paracoustics*

WhatsApps from Heaven

Bereavement in the Twenty-first Century

WhatsApps from Heaven

Bereavement in the Twenty-first Century

Louise Hamlin

BOOKS

Winchester, UK
Washington, USA

JOHN HUNT PUBLISHING

First published by O-Books, 2022
O-Books is an imprint of John Hunt Publishing Ltd., 3 East St., Alresford,
Hampshire SO24 9EE, UK
office@jhpbooks.com
www.johnhuntpublishing.com
www.o-books.com

For distributor details and how to order please visit the 'Ordering' section on our website.

Text copyright: Louise Hamlin 2021

ISBN: 978 1 78904 947 3
978 1 78904 948 0 (ebook)
Library of Congress Control Number: 2021944051

A CIP catalogue record for this book is available from the British Library.

Design: Stuart Davies

UK: Printed and bound by CPI Group (UK) Ltd, Croydon, CR0 4YY
Printed in North America by CPI GPS partners

We operate a distinctive and ethical publishing philosophy in
all areas of our business, from our global network of authors to
production and worldwide distribution.

Contents

For Patrick, with love

Acknowledgments

First and foremost, I would like to thank our children and their spouses. They too were bereaved. Patrick's children lost a much-loved father and grandfather; my children had already lost their own father two years before, and then lost their wonderful stepfather. I have only written about my own feelings in this book, but here I want to acknowledge that the children and their families also suffered a devastating loss, and their amazing care for me was all the more extraordinary. I thank them all from the bottom of my heart.

I would also like to thank all the friends and neighbours who have given me such tremendous support. As well as the friends mentioned in this book, others too have been unstintingly generous with their time and concern. I could not have managed to cope over the last two years without all the help that I have received. I realize how lucky I am in both family and friends.

Finally, I would like to thank Theresa Cheung, who responded to my original email when I felt I wanted the world to know about the signs that I was receiving from Patrick. She invited me on to her White Shores podcast and this gave me the confidence to carry on telling my story. She has been a guide and mentor, and encouraged me to write this book.

1

Introduction

This book is an account of a bereavement... a terrible, heartbreaking loss that destroyed the world as I knew it, and seemed to leave nothing but devastation in its wake. It is an account of the shock and the disbelief that lasted for many months. Although I knew rationally that my husband had died, emotionally I could not process it for at least a year, and my heart used to jump when I saw a Freelander car out of the corner of my eye, thinking for a nanosecond that it would be Patrick. For months I could not bear to take his clothes to a charity shop, because deep inside there was an almost subconscious feeling that he might return and need them. When I suddenly had a rush of blood to the head, bagged up all his shoes and deposited them at the local hospice shop all within the space of an hour, I returned home and sobbed and sobbed, because it seemed so final that he would not wear his boots again.

But now for the extraordinary part of this story. Slowly, very slowly, the grief became shot through with threads of joy because, against all expectation, I started to receive signs and messages from my deceased husband, signs which built to become totally irrefutable in my eyes. I say "against all expectation," because I have no religious faith, and had no fixed belief in an afterlife. Patrick and I spoke about dying when the end was near. He said that he wasn't scared, because either there was nothing at all, and that was nothing to fear, or, if there were something, he felt that he had led a good enough life for it to be all right for him. This was typical of the man—he was stoic in the extreme. He had had a fair measure of unhappiness in his life, but he never let it warp his spirit—he could always find a positive perspective and he bore the many slings and arrows of

1

outrageous fortune with fortitude.

We met in February 2005, two middle-aged divorcees, both with children in their twenties. Patrick was a successful London-based barrister and recorder (a part-time judge) and I, I was at a crossroads. I had lost my partner to cancer two years previously, and this had caused me to rethink my life and career. So, I had just given up an academic law career at Cambridge and I was wondering what to do next. What happened next was beyond my wildest dreams. I fell in love. Patrick was much more cautious with his feelings. Though I did not know it at first, he was clear in his own mind that he did not want a committed relationship, and he most certainly did not want to remarry. By the summer of 2005, his attitude had also become clear to me. I had been down the path of unrequited love in the past, and I did not want to take that road again, so with huge courage and a heavy heart, I told him that I was looking for love, and because he wasn't, I would say goodbye.

Of course, I hoped against hope that this would bring him to his senses (as I saw it), but for ten long weeks I waited to hear from him in vain. Then, at last, there was a phone call. Patrick was at a Chambers party, and obviously alcohol was flowing freely. Patrick was always a happy and cheerful drunk, and in his slightly inebriated state, he rang me to see how I was. I told him that I was going to go to India on holiday, and he suggested that I should come down to London and he would take me for an Indian, to acclimatize me. I went down, and this time, we both knew that we wanted a relationship. A year later we were living together. Four years later we married. Patrick used to say that it was the best wedding ever, and the happiest day of his life. Our marriage was truly wonderful, and our love for each other deepened with the years. We never took our happiness for granted, and we often used to look at each other, and say how incredibly lucky we were to have found each other. I had never expected to find love and nor had Patrick. They were the happiest days of our lives, by a country mile.

I can remember walking through the village where we lived one day, and just thinking to myself that it was so easy to be happy when you were in the right relationship. I felt totally blessed. My children were settled and had started to produce grandchildren, and Patrick's children were likewise happy and doing well in life. Patrick and I had a perfect life together, and we hoped that one day we would celebrate our silver wedding anniversary. It did not seem far-fetched. The only doubt was because I had a problem with my bone marrow—Patrick, on the other hand, was very strong and healthy. He had a brilliant immune system, and never fell prey to the colds and sniffles that I suffered every winter. According to some clever machine in the gym, he had the metabolism of a man 15 years younger, and his pulse rate was always way down in the 50s, while mine was up in the 80s. All in all, I knew that I would predecease Patrick, and to be frank, that was a great relief. I did not want to live without him. I did not want to outlive him.

So the sudden and totally unexpected diagnosis of bile duct cancer in November 2018 came as the most terrible shock. The following three months were a roller-coaster of hope and despair, sadly ending in the deepest despair imaginable. Even now I don't like to think about those last months of Patrick's life—the memories are too painful. But what seemed an ending turned out also to be a beginning, and my feelings of unutterable bleakness have now dissolved into something much more gentle and bearable. I now have a world-view that I would never have anticipated or predicted, and it is a world-view that I find very reassuring.

I hope that this true account of what happened to me will give you, the reader, pause for thought, and a realization that life is far more complex and extraordinary than we can imagine. And if you are bereaved, I hope that you will find a description of grieving which resonates, at least in part, with your experience, and so gives you some reassurance that what you are feeling is normal, and that you too can move in time through the depths of despair to a calmer and more peaceful place. And maybe this account will also help you more readily notice signs and messages that your loved ones are trying to send you.

Everything I write here—however extraordinary it may seem—is true; the only thing I have done is to change names, to protect people's privacy. I hope that my story gives you hope and reassurance.

2

Early Signs?

Patrick lost consciousness on 16 February 2019. He had been diagnosed with pneumonia the day before, and his breath was laboured and rattled through his poor wasted body. He lay in our bed, and I sat next to him, touching him. The children were all gathered around. We said our goodbyes and we kept vigil. The emergency doctor who came said that he would wait because death was only a few minutes away, but Patrick was strong and determined in life and in dying as well—he finally died, without gaining consciousness, on 18 February 2019. A man with a huge personality, and so much still to give, was no more. I was numb with shock. We all were.

The next few days passed in a blur; I just sat like a zombie, incapable of doing anything. I was totally bereft. I think that the combination of shock, which had been accumulating since that unexpected diagnosis three months previously, and of grief left me unable to function in any normal way. Our children and friends took over and allowed me just to sit blankly on the sofa. They put food in front of me at mealtimes, although I was not hungry and could barely eat. I had lost a stone and a half in the preceding three months, and I continued to lose weight because I had no appetite. The children started upon the grisly administration and paperwork that succeeds a death, while I answered questions with monosyllables and found it a huge effort to engage in any way with the perplexed grandchildren, or indeed with anyone or anything. I felt as if I were in a nightmare, which must surely come to an end…

I don't remember much of that time—just the odd vignette still sticks. I remember a retired vicar friend from another parish coming round shortly after Patrick's death, and my asking whether he believed in an afterlife. I didn't, or at least I didn't know, but I would have loved to, and I was genuinely interested in his answer. I was hoping that he would say something that would persuade me that our spirits survived our bodily death. He prevaricated and seemed quite uncomfortable with the question, and in the end came down to saying that there must be something, because otherwise there was no point to our life on this earth. I was so disappointed. I thought that answer said more about his life on earth than anything else, and I can also remember feeling surprised that he didn't seem to have a ready response to the question, even though a large part of his job must have involved talking to the newly-bereaved. Another cleric, to whom I went for support a few weeks later, again gave a very wishy-washy answer to the question. He said he thought that after death we walked in the hand of God. I asked him what on earth that meant, and he said he didn't know.

It was a couple of months later, when I was quietly weeping in the chapel of Addenbrooke's Hospital in Cambridge, that a chaplain came up to sit beside me and to talk. I asked him, with tears running down my face, if he believed in an afterlife, and I will never forget his response. "Oh," he said immediately, and with total conviction, "absolutely, 100% — I wouldn't be in this job otherwise. I certainly do." I still find it strange that, out of the three Church of England ministers whom I asked, only one seemed to truly believe that life continues after death — a basic tenet of Christianity. It must be uncomfortable to spend your professional life supporting ideas which you don't wholeheartedly endorse. But that hospital chaplain gave me hope, and I will be forever grateful to him for his certainty.

The Flame

Going back to February, it was just five days after Patrick had died that the first strange occurrence — or coincidence — took place. Jenny sent me the WhatsApp on the evening of 23

February. Jenny is a healer and friend. Her grandmother had been the village wise-woman and healer in a remote settlement in Northern Ireland, in the days before people could easily see or afford doctors, and the grandmother's touch seems to have skipped a generation and then been born again in Jenny. Jenny is very intelligent and had a university education and a "proper" job before she decided to follow her heart and learn about energy healing. She does something called bodywork, which is a little like reiki. She gently touches the body and channels energy to soften and heal. She has been giving me treatments for years, but Patrick was always sceptical about her work and thought that the effect she had upon me was probably placebo. (That is, of course, mysterious enough.) But—*in extremis*—Patrick asked for, or at least agreed to have, some sessions with Jenny while he lay gravely ill. She managed to give him just two sessions before he died. He changed his mind about her after the second—and unbeknownst to us, last—session that he had with her. He had been to an acupuncturist a few days before, but Jenny didn't know that, and it was not something that you would expect Patrick to have done, as he was very suspicious of complementary medicine. Anyway, Jenny was able to feel that he had had some energy work, and asked him about it. Patrick was very surprised by her realizing, and quite mystified. He mentioned to several people how extraordinary it was that she could tell.

So, anyway, I heard from Jenny as follows:

Dear Louise, I hope this is not out of order... but I have been meditating and thinking about Patrick. This morning I asked for a sign that he's ok. I asked to see fire (not in a fireplace) by the end of the day. So I went about my day and wasn't thinking of anything. I just went to close my curtains and there were flames in the garden opposite. It took my breath away as I had really set the idea aside. Anyway, I don't believe in coincidence, but I just wanted to share that with you. Lots of love and strength xxx

She sent a photograph of the flame with the WhatsApp.

I wanted to believe that it was a sign, but I suppose that, unlike Jenny, I do believe in coincidences—or, at least, I did then—so I felt rather ambivalent about it. It was certainly not enough to convince me of anything. I thought how wonderful it would be if Patrick were still alive in spirit, but I rather doubted that he was. Anyway, I rang up Jenny to ask her about it, and she was absolutely sure that Patrick had sent the unusual flame. And it was indeed strange—it was a very tall thin flame and it was difficult to imagine what had caused it. Unfortunately the fence between the gardens meant that it was not possible to see the source of the flame on the ground. Apparently, very soon after Jenny managed to photograph it, the flame died away.

Snowdrops

After our conversation, I was still confused. I did not know what to think—my heart wanted me to believe that it was a sign, but my head told me that it was just a coincidence. When I told Jenny how uncertain I was, she suggested that I should ask for a sign myself. I mulled over the idea, and decided that I would. So I asked Patrick to send me a bunch of snowdrops within the next three days. There was some history to the request. When my partner Rob had died in September 2002, I had, then too, wondered whether there was life after death, and, on prompting, I had again asked for a sign—that time, I had asked for sweet peas in a pot. The very next day, my close friend Karen had come round, bearing a bunch of sweet peas that she had picked from her garden and put in a jug made by me and given to her some years previously. I told her that I had asked Rob for a pot of sweet peas, and she said that she had felt impelled to pick them—they were the last of the season—

and then she had felt drawn to the pot I had made. Rob had liked Karen and so it made sense that he would have tried to influence her. But I was unable to believe that this was anything more than a coincidence, and I had forgotten all about it until Jenny suggested I should ask for a sign.

It was still in February, and snowdrops were in season, so mine was not an outlandish request. Two days later, my dear friend Anna came to stay. She came armed with food and love, but she didn't bring snowdrops or any other flowers. After my three day ultimatum to Patrick was up, I told Anna what I had asked for, and how disappointed I was that the request had not been answered. She put her head in her hands. Apparently she had gone to a farmers' market the day before coming to stay, and she had passed a stall selling snowdrops. She had had a really strong impulse to buy some for me, but she had resisted, thinking—quite correctly—that I would have a lot of flowers already. "Patrick was probably saying to me, *buy the snowdrops for Louise, Anna, just buy the sodding snowdrops*, and I didn't," she moaned. "And I wanted to, but I thought it was stupid!" That made me laugh—the first time for ages.

The Funeral and Cheap Trick

Patrick's funeral was on 4 March 2019. There was standing room only in the church. People from all walks of life turned up to pay their respects because Patrick had the widest circle of friends of anyone I know—he might have been a successful lawyer, but he was also friends with a whole range of people from every imaginable background. He treated everyone absolutely the same—and never paid the slightest attention to whether or not people had money or status. He just noticed whether they were good-hearted and authentic, whether he liked them or not. That was one of the things I loved about him. He teased, insulted and was rude to everyone equally. He argued with everyone equally. Quite often, I wished he wouldn't...

I survived the funeral in a sort of dream, and barely noticed that the children thoughtfully stood around me and protected me during the wake that followed in the Village Hall. I smiled, cried and let myself be kissed, and was on total autopilot.

Jenny again features in this story. When she was driving home from the funeral, she decided to ask for another sign. She asked to hear *I Want You to Want Me* by Cheap Trick, on the radio. It was a song from the 80s, and she had never heard it being broadcast, and so she was deliberately choosing something obscure. She didn't hear it on her drive home, but the next morning she went to meet her parents, who were visiting, at the local railway station, and as she stood on the platform, the song came over the Tannoy. It gave her quite a shock, and also delighted her. She was sure it was a sign from Patrick, and she felt that Patrick was being very playful and laughing with her. He had had a great sense of humour. She hurried to tell me, but again, I thought it could just be coincidence. I longed for proof that he was still alive in spirit, but I needed something more definite than that.

The White Feather

The dreary days went by, and it took all my energy to get up and take Phoebe, our spaniel, for a walk. Otherwise, I existed in a strange and timeless place. The children came to stay with me, and then I went to stay with them, because I couldn't bear to be in the house by myself, but I was restless, and never stayed anywhere for very long. When I was away, I wanted to be at home, and when I was at home, I couldn't cope and wanted to go away. I happened to be staying with one of my sons on Monday, 18 March 2019, a month after Patrick had died. It seemed significant that a whole month had passed, and in my misery, I decided to ask for another sign. It was mid-afternoon, and I was lying on the bed in my son's attic. By now, I had read about feathers coming to the bereaved, and so I decided to ask for a white feather. Nothing happened. That did not surprise me. I felt despondent and the lack of a feather only confirmed to me that there were no signs, and death meant the end of a person, however vital that person had been in life.

The next morning, a friend sent me a WhatsApp with an unusual message. She wanted to tell me that she had been gardening in the spring sunshine the previous afternoon, and she had been thinking of Patrick and me, when two soft white downy feathers had floated down right in front of her. It was sufficiently peculiar for her to want me to know. I had not been in touch with her for some days, and so she had absolutely no idea that I had been asking for a feather that same afternoon, or indeed at any time. Also, this was not the type of WhatsApp that she normally sent. Her messages were usually down-to-earth and practical.

The Bedside Lights

Two weeks later, Karen, my friend of the sweet peas who had also been close to both of us, got in touch. On Saturday, 6 April 2019, she found her two bedside lights had been turned on during the day in her empty house. She could find no rational explanation. She was absolutely sure that she had not turned them on herself—it had been light outside when she had got up, and there was no need to turn on any light, let alone the lights on both sides of the double bed. To do that, she would have had to walk round the bed to turn on the further light. No one else had been in the house. Her husband was away, and she had spent the whole day in her studio in the garden. She felt very strongly that it was Patrick. I was pleased to hear this, but the part of me that wanted to believe began to feel a little peeved that all these possible signs seemed to come via friends rather than directly to me. I occasionally felt wonderful sensations of love and peace, during these first two months after his death, but I still had not had a concrete sign myself. To be fair, I hadn't asked, other than as I have described above, partly because I didn't want to be a nuisance if, as books suggested, his spirit had things to do, and partly because most of me did not really believe in the signs anyway. As the weeks went by, however, and as I read more and more about the afterlife, I questioned myself—and the universe—and I decided to be more proactive.

The Feather on the Train

So, on 3 May, feeling I wanted something tangible, I asked Patrick for a feather on a train—I had four train journeys booked over the following two days. That afternoon, I took a train, and, unsurprisingly, there was no feather. The next day, I caught a second train. It was quite full but I spotted a pair of empty seats and made my way there. I sat down and then glanced at the vacant seat next to me—and there, just lying unobtrusively on the seat, was a small grey feather. The seats were upholstered in some sort of foam, and there was no sensible explanation as to the feather being there. I did not know what to think. Again, I thought it could be coincidence—though it did seem odd. By now, I was writing down in a notebook possible signs from Patrick, so I picked the feather up and later stuck it into my book. I really wanted to believe that some sort of spirit, who was consciously Patrick, existed, and as the "coincidences" built up, I became more willing to think that maybe Patrick was sending signs. My belief that life ended at death was being shaken by this succession of events. But most of me still thought that coincidence was a possible explanation for the unusual incidents, and maybe there had been an electric fault with the bedside lights. I did not know it, but I would have to wait until the end of June for the first extraordinary signs to appear.

3

Living in the Moment

Patrick had been my great love and, without him, I felt totally bereft. I felt as though a part of me had been violently torn away, leaving a gaping wound and only half a person. To my surprise, the sun kept on rising and setting, even though Patrick was no more in the world, and other people even carried on their business as though nothing cataclysmic had happened. Not that I had any interest in their business—I was totally uninterested in anything external to my grief.

I was also tired. Actually, tired is not strong enough a word. I felt completely exhausted, and even managing to clean my teeth in the morning was an achievement. I knew that I was just holding on by my fingertips, and actually, I would not have minded losing my grip on reality or even dying. In my darkest moments, I felt that I would welcome death, because then I would either experience oblivion or I would be reunited with my husband.

So I had to work out a coping strategy, and I discovered that it was to live in the moment. I tried to ensure that I had something in my diary for every single day, so that the day was broken up into manageable segments. I never had to survive for more than three or four hours at a time. And then I would just concentrate on getting through those three or four hours. I did not let myself think about the future—even thinking about tomorrow was too much, too bleak. And I most certainly could not let myself think about the past, because then what I had lost would be thrown into vivid relief. But I could think about the present—the little chunk of time that I had to pass through before something else happened.

Living in the moment helped me through the first most

painful months and, gradually, I was able to live in larger chunks of time, and slowly, slowly I could begin to think about the coming week or month. To start with, I felt as though I was walking a tightrope over a deep ravine. I just had to keep my nerve and look straight ahead, and then I was okay. If I looked down, I was lost. If I tried to look too far ahead, I would also lose my balance and fall, but on the tightrope, with little careful steps, I was surviving. As the weeks and months passed, I became much more adept on the tightrope—I found that I could glance down and keep my balance, and I could look around without falling. The tightrope itself slowly became wider, so I could stride rather than creep. It is trite to say that time is the great healer, but with time, my balance improved.

I also used living in the moment to help me answer the constant question, "How are you?" I found it tricky because I knew that usually the questioner just wanted me to say "fine", but I couldn't. I wasn't, and it almost seemed disrespectful to Patrick to say that I was. So I would reply, "Well, I am taking it a day at a time," and that would allow the other person to move on, feeling that the social niceties had been complied with, while I felt that I had answered honestly.

4

Photographs

Photographs of Patrick also helped me a lot. After he died, I wanted to surround myself with photographs, both of him and of the two of us together. There were not all that many of the latter—I had tended to take photos of him, and he of me, but we had rarely asked someone else to take a photograph of the both of us and we were not of the generation that takes selfies. Luckily, I did have one particularly good picture of us both, dating back to 2017. We had gone to a special hotel for lunch, to celebrate our wedding anniversary, and we went to sit outside on the terrace for coffee. It was a warm, sunny day and we had just eaten a delicious meal. The terrace looked over an extensive lawn, and we were laughing about the first time we had been to the hotel, when Phoebe was a puppy. We had taken her for a walk over this immaculate lawn, in front of everyone on the terrace, when she suddenly had the most dreadful diarrhoea, so runny that it was impossible to bag up. I was horrified. We tried to pretend that nothing untoward had happened and just hoped that nobody had noticed. Then dragging Phoebe behind

us, we beat a hasty retreat. Seven years later, as we sat there, we remembered the episode, and we were just laughing about it when a couple sitting nearby asked the waiter to take a picture. I decided to do the same. I can vividly remember my thought process: when we were old and grey, in a far distant future, it would be lovely to look back and remember a happy day on Dartmoor. I could see, in my mind's eye, an ancient Louise and Patrick sitting on the sofa together and fondly reminiscing while looking at pictures from the past.

So shortly after Patrick died, when I was pretty incapable of doing anything, one of my sons arranged the printing of lots of photographs. I placed them all around the house. Wherever I went inside, I could see a picture of Patrick and I could talk to him and tell him that I loved him. I put a photograph of a smiling Patrick in the summerhouse, and I greeted him every time I went up there. I found it immensely comforting to be surrounded by his image, almost as if he were still around.

The difficulty came some 18 months later, when I began to realize that I did not want to turn the house into a shrine, and that there were probably too many photographs of Patrick for comfort. The problem was, I did not know how to deal with it. I did not want to consign his image to a drawer. At the time, I was sending paintings to friends of Patrick. He had wanted friends to choose a painting, but the whole process had been very drawn out, first because of waiting for probate and then of course lockdown had stymied plans. I eventually started to dispatch the paintings in the late summer of 2020, and with each painting I sent one of the framed photographs of Patrick. That reduced the number on display without my feeling uncomfortable. Then, a month or two later, I found that, after all, I could put some of the photographs in a cupboard. Now, I still have several photographs of him in the house, and I still chat to them and smile at them, but the number is no longer excessive. At least, I don't think so.

5

Mediums

"Mediums never help—they are never totally accurate," pontificated a bereavement counsellor whom I went to see a little while after Patrick had died. "Don't go to see a medium," he said. I was a little surprised by his attitude, because he was a cleric, but I have since learned that the Anglican Church (and probably other denominations as well) has a fairly uneasy relationship with self-help as far as mediums are concerned. By the time of my counselling session, I had already been to see a medium—actually two or three—and I had found huge comfort in what they said, but as I did not feel strong enough to disagree with the counsellor, I stayed silent.

I quite understand why people may be worried about mediums—of course, there are going to be charlatans out there, just as there are crooked lawyers and dishonest plumbers. People who visit mediums are likely to be grieving and/or vulnerable, so it is possible that mediumship attracts more than its fair share of predators, but that of itself should not throw the whole concept into disrepute. The important thing is to keep your wits about you, however distressed you are, and if you are uncertain, take a sensible friend with you as a witness and support.

In the weeks after Patrick died I had a deep and visceral need to touch my husband, to hug him, to talk to him, to laugh with him, to hold his hand, and of course I could do none of these things. But a medium could possibly provide some sort of contact with him, and that was what I craved, and so I went to see, or I rang, several. This, even though I was not sure what I believed.

To check that they were kosher, and so I could properly

assess their abilities, I was careful never to reveal more than the basic fact that my husband had died in February. I never gave any more information. When I went to see a medium, I just wore my normal clothes—tatty jeans and a well-loved jumper. Patrick used to say that I scrubbed up well, but that is probably because he was comparing me to my daily look, which featured old clothes and no make-up. Of course, as soon as I opened my mouth it would be possible to identify my background, and those mediums who saw me in person would also be able to note my demeanour and general aura of being middle-class. For this reason, I was never impressed by generic comments like, "Oh, your husband is here and he's well-spoken, intelligent, well-educated and successful." One would not need a psychic ability to guess that he would have been all of that. Likewise, when I was told that he was sending lots of love, I liked to hear it, but did not give much credence to that by itself. I was unlikely to be consulting a medium if I had not loved my husband, and felt loved by him. However, when a medium told me that my husband "loved me to bits," then I believed her. Whenever Patrick had wanted to get on with his work, his way of getting me to disappear was to say, "Love you to bits, now bugger off!" Equally, a medium who saw him with books did not impress me, but the medium who described him in a room with a lot of law books, did.

The first medium I saw was not a success. She began by saying that she had a military man, and did that make sense? I said that it did not. She carried on, and nothing resonated with me, so I kept on answering, "no," to her every question. In the end, she became rather irritated by my repeatedly denying any truth to what was being said, and she then started to blame me for being too closed. I was unimpressed. But, I was not going to let one dud reading prevent me from persevering, and so I made contact with several more.

I had another problematic reading—this time with a well-known American medium, on a video call. She said things which did not ring true to my English ears. She said that Patrick was saying to her "the Lord is..." I interrupted to say that Patrick would never have spoken about "the Lord." She insisted that he had, and it made me realize that spirit communication is mediated through the cultural norms of the medium, and that this can cause distortion. She also said that Patrick was living in a little cottage in the countryside. Maybe this was also a matter of cultural distortion. For some reason, Patrick had a deep-rooted prejudice against cottages, and if anyone ever called our house "a cottage," he was apoplectic.

So I discounted the mediums who did not convince me. On the other hand, I also had some extraordinary readings, which defied all logic and reason, and these were wonderful. Patrick really did seem to be present and communicating through the medium, and I felt overjoyed.

16 February

For example, in April, two months after Patrick had died, I searched the Internet for a medium and then rang her to ask for a reading. I just said that I was Louise and that my husband had died in February. Nothing more. She said, "Hmm, that may be a bit early... He died in the middle of February, didn't he?" I replied, "Yes." She then stated, quite firmly, "Oh, he died on the 16th of February." I replied that he had lost consciousness on the 16th, but that he had actually died on the 18th. "Well," she replied, without hesitation, "he's telling me that he died on the 16th! And so that's what I am going to write down." I was very impressed by this—she did not know me from Adam, and she had no means of knowing when Patrick had died. She then carried on by saying that my love had kept my husband alive longer than he should have lived and that she was getting a lot of love from him to me and that he was not a gentleman who entered relationships easily. The last comment was indeed true, and it seemed a funny thing to say straight away on the phone. It was not something one could have guessed.

Cornflowers and Slippers

I did not have to wait long to travel to see this medium in person because she had just had a cancellation, and so I saw her two days later. She described Patrick—both his appearance and his personality—very accurately and I felt much comforted. It was later, on another occasion when I went to see her again, that she said he was giving me cornflowers—and she asked why he was doing that. I understood at once. My grandfather had grown cornflowers, and throughout the summer he used to wear a fresh cornflower in his buttonhole every day—he was a bit of a dandy. So when we had married, just nine years previously, I had asked Patrick to wear a cornflower in his buttonhole, in memory of my grandfather. He, his best man and all the ushers wore blue cornflowers, and we had one preserved in a paperweight.

She then said that he was pointing at his feet, which were in slippers, and laughing. That I also understood. I had sent the undertaker Patrick's country gear to wear in the coffin, because I thought that he was at his happiest when outside, but instead of shoes, I had sent his slippers, because I thought they would be more comfortable for him. It was a slightly odd combination.

Another thing she said made no sense at all to me at the time, but in retrospect, I realize that it was telling. She said that Patrick was surrounded by birds and birdsong. I will write about birds later.

There were a couple of other things which I could not make sense of. She asked if I knew a Peter who had passed, and I said no. As I type this now, however, I realize that I actually knew two Peters who had died some two or three years before, but I didn't recall either of them at the time. I regret now that I denied them. Another strange thing was that she saw Patrick on a boat, tying knots. I still do not find any resonance with that, because although he had been a sea cadet as a teenager, he never really enjoyed sailing—largely because he suffered from seasickness. It seemed wrong. But the date of death, or at least of dying to the world, the cornflowers and the slippers, as well as the very accurate description of Patrick, all this seemed true and persuasive. These were details that she could not possibly have guessed. I found huge comfort and consolation in seeing this medium. And it occurred to me then that a medium does not have to be totally accurate to be still amazingly and uncannily convincing.

Picasso

In those first few weeks, I had some healing sessions with different energetic healers. I did not approach them for mediumship but because I felt so broken inside, and gentle energetic healing seemed a positive and easy thing I could do for myself. I discovered that many energetic healers also have some psychic or medium-like powers—at least, several said that they could feel my husband's spirit around me as they worked on me. The really weird thing is that two different healers told me that Patrick was saying he had met Picasso. The first time, I just mentally shrugged my shoulders and ignored it, because after all I had not come to connect with Patrick, but for energy work. I wrote it down in my notebook, as I wrote everything down, and then forgot all about it. But then, strangely, some time later, another healer suddenly asked if my husband had liked art. "Why are you asking?" I queried, feeling rather bemused by the question. "Well," he said, "I can feel your husband's here, and he's just told me that he has been hanging out with Picasso!" It rang a vague bell with me, and that evening I went back through my notebook and found, yes, I had been told that before. To put this in context, I should say that no other famous person has ever been mentioned in any reading that I have had. Either it was an extraordinary coincidence, or maybe, just maybe, there was something to it. I could imagine that Patrick would be thrilled to hang out with Picasso. He had been very interested in art, and indeed as a hobby he bought paintings and then sold them over the Internet. Unfortunately, he was very good at the purchasing side, and rather less successful at the selling, so we had masses of framed paintings propped up against any spare wall. It used to drive me mad.

Orbs and Flowers

Towards the end of May, I felt ready to see another medium—I just wanted to know that Patrick was around and I wanted to hear that he was happy. I was given the contact details of a medium called Maria who was only about 50 minutes' drive away, and so I sent her a WhatsApp to ask for an appointment. This was on a Thursday evening, and I was going to France in a week's time, so I was delighted when she replied that she could see me the next morning. When I arrived, she explained what had happened. Apparently, just as she received my WhatsApp, her sitting room lit up with orbs of light, and she knew this was a sign that she had to see me straight away—so, bless her, she postponed her two Friday morning appointments so that she could see me instead. She videoed the orbs on her phone and showed me—it was spectacular. She said it was my husband and he was coming over so strongly because of the strength of his bond with me—he was coming on a great wave of love.

She also spoke about all the flowers that he was giving me, and this has been a recurring theme with the mediums I have seen. I suppose that a cynic would say that it was a good bet that a husband would have given his wife flowers, but Patrick was a particularly prolific flower-giver. He had a good story about the time he went to the local florists to order some flowers and he mentioned that they were for his wife. The young assistant looked very surprised, and rather indiscreetly (and naively) exclaimed, "Oh, we didn't think you were married. We were discussing it and we thought you must be Internet-dating because you buy so many flowers!"

Maria will feature again in my account, because somehow she seems to be a portal that Patrick can use to contact me. She is a down-to-earth wife and mother, who has always been psychic and aware of the deceased, but who resisted being "different" for many years, and instead pursued a career as a primary school teacher. She sometimes did readings for friends, but was reluctant to read for money. A few months before I saw her, she decided she could resist no more and that she would read for other people as well. As she hardly charged anything, she was not doing it for financial gain, but because she felt impelled to help the bereaved and those who want to contact "the other side." My reading with her was wonderful—I really felt that Patrick was there in spirit.

Green Earrings

The last medium I saw was recommended by a friend, who had been blown away by what had been said to her. I booked both a reading and a healing session, and drove there with high hopes—it was a two hour journey, but my friend said it would be well worth it. When I arrived, I explained that Patrick had died in February, and the medium, Rosemary, said that as it was only five months since the death, she did not know if Patrick would be able to come in. She then started to explain that she liked to do the healing first before the mediumship. But she suddenly interrupted herself to say that a gentleman (and Patrick was indeed a gentleman) had suddenly come in with a very strong energy and was very impatient. "Oh my goodness," she exclaimed, "I have to do the reading now! He doesn't want to wait!" She said that he had come in with a classic smell, and asked if I had ever smelt him. As it happened, I had been lying in bed a few days before, and I had suddenly and unmistakeably smelt his aftershave. Rosemary said that it was difficult for a spirit to send smells, and he was probably just learning how to do it.

The reading was simply lovely for me, full of love and gratitude. Some funny little details stand out. Rosemary said that Patrick loved it when I wore my green earrings. This apparently random comment made perfect sense. He had given me a pair of beautiful emerald earrings when we had got engaged, and I always wore them "for best". They were very special. Then she said, "Patrick says to check the curtain poles." I have no idea whether it was coincidental but a few months later the curtain pole in the kitchen suddenly fell to the ground with a deafening crash — the plastic bracket had deteriorated and failed.

Another thing she said, and this was very welcome, was that Patrick was telling me to drink good wine. This would obviously not impress a cynic, but I could imagine him saying it. One of the last things he did before he died was to order three cases of good red wine — and as he himself only drank white, this was in effect a leaving present.

Dr Gary Schwartz described in his book, *The Afterlife Experiments*, how he conducted double- and treble-blind experiments with mediums, and that the results showed some people do indeed seem to be able to communicate with the deceased. I find his writing compelling, and the examples he gives are truly breathtaking. But even more compelling is my experience. Mediums have said things to me that I feel came directly from Patrick, and cannot be explained in any other way. I suspect that in the future more and more people will recognise that there are some blessed souls amongst us who have special and wonderful powers. I am very grateful that there are. I have not been to see a medium for nearly a year now, because I have not felt the need, but I found the good mediums gave me huge reassurance and consolation in the early months after Patrick's death. I found that, slowly, I was beginning to believe a little more fully in an afterlife, and in spirit communication. In the popular tradition of cognitive dissonance, however, part of me was still very doubtful.

6

The Montblanc Pen

By the end of May, three months after Patrick had died, I had had a few possible signs from him, but nothing that totally convinced me. The matter of the disappearing pen is a case in point.

I had bought a large new address book because for some reason I wanted to begin again with addresses, and to fill it with the contact details of everyone who was important to me or had been important to Patrick. I usually write with disposable fine-tipped pens—I buy a box of 12 at a time and distribute them around the house and in my car and pockets, so that I am never without a pen when I need one. But some years ago, I treated myself to a Montblanc fountain pen, which I only used rarely but enjoyed writing with on special occasions. I thought that my new address book was one such occasion, and so I went to my desk and collected my Montblanc pen to use.

I sat down at the kitchen table and started. I had reached the H's when my neighbour Fiona turned up with supper. Fiona is a wonderful neighbour who frequently fed me in the first few months of my bereavement because she realized that I had no interest in feeding myself. I shall always be grateful to her. Anyway, when she arrived, I stopped writing and stood up to collect some cutlery and plates. She made a space by pushing the address book and my pen along the table, and we sat down to eat. The kitchen table is over six feet long. It had originally been in the dining hall of one of the Inns of Court, and the boards are meant to have come from ships that fought in the Armada. I don't know if they were Spanish or English ships, but either way, the oak is very old and beautiful. In the 1980s, the Inn of Court decided to sell the original tables and to make replicas, because the originals were too heavy for the staff to move easily. Patrick bought one of the tables when he was still married to his first wife. She kept it after the divorce, but many years later, when she was about to move house, Patrick bought it from her. Patrick used to enjoy complaining that he had had to buy the table twice over. We put it in the kitchen.

Anyway, Fiona and I had supper, and she went home. I went to bed. The next morning, I couldn't find the pen. I asked Fiona if she had picked it up, but she said she had merely pushed it to one side. Despite searching and searching, the pen has never reappeared.

I could not understand what had happened to it. Fiona, I should say, is a very close, trustworthy and long-standing friend, and there is no way that she would have surreptitiously picked up and stolen the pen. I was totally bemused. It occurred to me that if Patrick had somehow taken my Montblanc, he was being very clever because I was always going to notice its disappearance. Had he taken one of my cheap pens, I would not have clocked that it had vanished. I would have put one down unthinkingly and then, if it were not to hand, I would just have helped myself to a new one. The fact that the fountain pen vanished from the table into thin air seemed quite remarkable. I also thought it was relevant that Patrick always liked to write with a fountain pen—he had no time for my cheap disposable ones. I was beginning to suspect that my materialist outlook was quite inadequate to explain what was happening around me, though I still harboured doubts.

Some months later, Patrick caused two more dematerialisations, and this time I had much less doubt about them. Again, they were extremely clever, involving Rizla papers and a playing card.

7

Meditation

All this time, I was trying to cope with my feelings. I was totally numb at first, and then I began to feel as though I had a large, dark, deep lake inside me. I felt that I had lost all boundaries, and had become an amorphous liquid blob. This was scary and unpleasant, and even more so because the lake churned away and gave me no peace.

As well as an unutterable sadness, I felt a maelstrom of other emotions, including guilt. I blamed myself that I hadn't insisted that Patrick have a full medical when he turned 70; I worried that I had caused the bile duct cancer because I had given him too many supplements; I blamed myself that my love for him hadn't been strong enough to see him through the illness. I somehow felt that it must be my fault, and this anguish was not susceptible to reason.

I soon found that the summerhouse was my refuge. It is a

The Summer House

long way up a steeply sloping garden, in what purports to be a wild flower meadow (this is a work in progress), and it looks out on the wide bowl of a valley, with pasture and trees, and above all, sky. You can't see any houses, or hear human noise from its eyrie, and I would carry out a chair and just sit for hours staring at the view. I realized that I didn't feel lonely up at the summerhouse, unlike in the house itself which now only echoed with silence and loss.

I discovered, almost by accident as I sat quietly in nature up at the top of the garden, that meditating helped assuage the churning, and so that is what I started to do. At the same time, I was busy reading everything that I could find about the afterlife, and one recurring theme in the books was that meditation would help raise one's vibrations and make one more receptive to contact by spirits. I was not exactly sure what it meant to raise one's vibrations—I just gathered that it was to do with one's energy—but I was anxious to have any possible contact with Patrick if he had survived in spirit, and so that was a further reason to meditate daily.

I began to look for specific advice about meditation, and discovered that there was a whole industry out there, teaching people how to meditate, when to meditate and what to meditate on. There was a plethora of downloads, CDs, courses and books. The trouble was, there seemed to be no consensus as to how to start or carry on. Every teacher seemed to have slightly different advice, and it was hard to know which to follow. Some years ago, when I was lonely and unhappy, I had done a course on transcendental meditation, but then I had met Patrick and I had lost interest. Apart from repeating a mantra, I could not really remember what you did. So I decided to go my own way, and just sit quietly. I would try to calm my mind by being aware of my breath. Sometimes I would just breathe very gently and lightly in a circular motion. Other times, I would imagine my out-breath driving down through the molecules towards my deep core, and then my in-breath taking in air from that low level. In that way, I found I could go deeper and deeper into my being. I also found it helpful to repeat the old mantra from long ago, or more often, just to count "one, two, three," over and over again. Only rarely did I manage to clear my mind for more than a few moments, but, even so, I found a respite in meditation that I had found nowhere else.

I do not know whether it was because I was meditating, for an hour or more every day, that I was able to receive the signs that Patrick sent. I do not know whether I was more alert to the less obvious signs—the feathers for example—because I was meditating. All I can say with certainty is that meditating helped me and continues to do so. It calms me and gives me an inner peace. I should also mention here that sometimes when I meditate I start jerking uncontrollably—my shoulders in particular go up and down in a violent shrug. I interpret this as the meditation releasing physical and emotional blocks in my body, and when the jerking subsides I find that I feel particularly calm.

8

First WhatsApps

The first strange WhatsApps took me completely by surprise. It was on a warm, sunny afternoon towards the end of June that I locked the front door, poured myself a mug of tea, and went up to my refuge in the summerhouse. Phoebe came with me. She loves it up there in the field and keeps busy following scents and digging for... I know not what... but she certainly likes digging. I was recently back home from France and I was still finding it lonely in the house, but out in nature by the summerhouse, I felt calmer and nearer to Patrick. That morning, Maria had sent me a WhatsApp asking how I was. She typed that she had been moved by my grief, and continued by describing her gran's death, when she interrupted herself to say that she was being distracted by a man in a legal wig. She made a joke about it, and then felt mortified when I answered that Patrick had been a barrister—she hadn't known that he was a lawyer.

I sat and drank my tea, and then meditated to calm the churning that I still felt inside. After an hour or so, I went back down to the house. The house was as I had left it, quite silent. There was no radio on or anything like that. No one could have entered the house. So when I looked at my phone, which I had left in the kitchen, I was surprised to see a whole lot of gibberish, in the WhatsApp message box ready to send to Maria. It didn't make any sense, and I couldn't work out how on earth it had got there. It was as follows:

Gov 5 verse vermont cough von va nerve rah rah rah rah rah rah ear air air u wretch choi choice says n or nor uh n earn no or wars wii each woop cocker kaka cuckoo uh took ooh ooh ooh ooh ooh ooh ooh new choice choi choo oi oi choo joy joy ca chevy coat shot potter otter are of it it's solicit mirror in ri uh interest sister ossett hrithik penh th wanna wanna newfield 400 til th tot otter ish ithaca off thin winner of thin what shifts thin should tricia in should ru what theatre chore yunis of theron in orinda of doll ro assists sorensen rah nj tint rah tint frost rah todd tot lear lear tip fiddler kick kisser fisher id pier if na enlighten popper referral warts after til slur fl where lair chair hurry mull preferably hair brett hair tn hence bre better baboon tha we're we'd tidworth quick v til tutor it' is eternity l will well or or where's wa yah where f sri lanka where care th court lob todd buena le uh we're amphibian of.

To start with, I was inclined to delete it, but then I thought again, and decided to send it to Maria and ask what she thought. She replied that she had no idea, but perhaps it was a sign from Patrick?

The next day, 21 June 2019, Maria sent this WhatsApp:

Darling Blenheim cotta les Veela bin hi Sri Lanka le omelette darling it's me grid loots libb prob see meant too bee alias draft herenismo see le auamanons darling it's me happily lillies fifth route memories darling it's me Valentine's Day 2019 darling it's me

She added underneath,

Louise I was just going to message you I don't know why but felt I needed to this was ready to send to you and I have no clue what he or what it means it doesn't make sense I don't know if u can get the gist of it.

I didn't know what to think. On the one hand, it seemed magical and wonderful if indeed the repeated message "darling it's me" meant that Patrick was sending me a WhatsApp. And certainly he always called me darling. On the other hand, it seemed so incredible and I wondered if Maria was playing some strange joke on me. She seemed like a perfectly sensible, grounded and well-intentioned woman, but perhaps I had misread her? Valentine's Day 2019 had been one of the last days of Patrick's life and he had sent me a dozen red roses and a touching card, but why Sri Lanka was mentioned, I had no idea. I couldn't really believe that Maria had made it up, but I was unable to accept with certainty that the message had come from Patrick.

On 1 July, I received another strange WhatsApp, apparently from Maria.

18022019darling ggjyol uplift
7yearsmessgeonboarddgrrejgunexgxcfaawrjlopppg

Here is the following exchange:

Louise: *Did you send this to me Maria?*
Maria: *Hi Louise what is it ? not come from me I'm having my worktops fitted so we are in the garden unpacking kitchen boxes xx*
Louise: *It apparently came from you via WhatsApp !!! Xx*
Maria: *Louise sorry it did I've just looked but I don't understand it as we have been outside and my phone was in the house xx*
Louise: *OMG! So do you think it's Patrick?? Can you make any sense of it? Xxx*
Maria: *That message means nothing to me at all it's like a barcode or something those numbers xx*

Now in fact the numbers 18022019 were the date of Patrick's death, but I had never told Maria exactly when he had died —I had just told her that he had died in February, and I deliberately asked her if she could make sense of the message to see if she had somehow discovered his date of death and sent me the WhatsApp. Again, I believed her but at the same time didn't know what to believe. I just wanted something more certain, and not involving a third party. True, Maria could not have written the first message, the one that I found on my phone, but thereafter she could have made it all up—though that seemed as improbable as Patrick sending the messages. I was perplexed.

I quite often felt that he was near me, but I couldn't really trust my feelings. I still needed an indubitable sign—and that was what arrived a few weeks later. At last, I was to receive a sign that I really could not doubt. Before that, however, I would like to discuss bereavement counselling.

Bereavement Counselling

After Patrick died, I knew that I needed all the help I could find, and so I looked for bereavement counselling. I discovered that there was a lot of such help available; some was provided free by charities and the local hospice, and other counsellors charged, but always reasonably (though I do live in a rural area, a long way from London). This was in 2019, pre-COVID, and I suspect that it is much harder to find free counselling nowadays, and no doubt there are long waiting lists.

The first two or three counsellors I tried were very worthy and kind, but not particularly helpful. Years ago, when I was at Cambridge, I had been appointed a tutor, which meant that I was given pastoral responsibilities. I felt totally unqualified to help students with emotional or psychological problems, and so I enrolled on a counselling course, and for one day a year (albeit an academic year) I gathered with some fifteen others to learn how to be a counsellor. We were taught not to offer advice, but merely to reflect back what the client was saying. I did not particularly agree with this approach, because there were times when I felt I could add something worthwhile to the conversation, but that would certainly have been frowned upon by our teachers. So when I saw the first bereavement counsellors, and they sat there, and let me cry, and reflected back to me what I was saying through my tears, I knew that they had been taught the same protocol. Frankly, I did not find it helpful. One of them, from a charity, came to my house, which was kind of her. She eyed the books on my coffee table, books about whether or not there was an afterlife, and baldly said, as she sat down to start the session, "He's not coming back, you know." I did not find that very helpful either. I was also slightly surprised, because she professed to be a practising Christian and wore a cross round her neck. She was a volunteer, and presumably her volunteering had something to do with her Christian faith, but she obviously had no truck with the afterlife.

So I continued to cast about, and I contacted someone whom I found on the Internet. She was a general counsellor rather than a specialist in bereavement, but I thought that she was worth a go—especially as she lived quite near to me. She was wonderful. She would make me a coffee, and we would sit in her living room on comfy chairs, and talk. When she heard I had a dog, she suggested I should bring Phoebe with me—she had a dog as well. So Phoebe would turn up to, and rush straight to the kitchen where she knew she would be given a treat. Then both dogs would settle down at our feet and we would chat. Suzy would listen to me, and make sure she understood what I was trying to say, but then she would say what she thought, and what her experiences were. It was so very refreshing to talk to a counsellor who contributed to the conversation, so that we had a dialogue, rather than a monologue which just ricocheted back to me. I found our sessions really helpful. Suzy was like a friend, but a friend that I could offload on week after week without feeling the slightest bit guilty.

I began to tell her about the signs that I was getting, and she took me seriously and believed me, even though she found it difficult to accommodate what I was saying with her world-view. When I then started to read about quantum physics, to try to understand my experiences, she offered to contact her brother, a physicist, with my questions, and he replied as best he could.

I carried on seeing Suzy until lockdown for COVID intervened, and I will keep in touch with her in the future. I was lucky, and I found a counsellor who really helped me come through my grief. I hope others are lucky like that too.

Now for these WhatsApp groups…

10

The WhatsApp Groups

Despite the precursors, I was totally dumbfounded by the most extraordinary of all Patrick's signs, a sign that arrived on 6 August 2019, his daughter's birthday.

I was staying with one of my sons and his family in Balham, and that morning I took Phoebe for a walk on Tooting Common as usual. The common is near their home and it is very popular with dog walkers and joggers. Phoebe knows it quite well and I usually walk around for half an hour or so and then put her back on the lead and return to the house. The day was dry and cloudy with sunny intervals—although it was August it was cool enough to need a jacket and I had poo bags in one pocket and my phone in another. It was just a normal sort of day.

Halfway through the walk, I sat down on a bench and sent a WhatsApp to Patrick's daughter, wishing her a happy birthday. I can remember that I thought carefully about what to say, because it was obviously a very bittersweet day for her, and I wanted to acknowledge her grief and her loss while also sending her my love. The message was sent at 11.04am and I then got up from the bench, put the phone back in my pocket and carried on walking. I remember hoping that Patrick was aware that I was trying to support his daughter.

When I got back home, I pulled out my phone and was astonished to see two notifications—it said that I had created two WhatsApp groups, both at 11.06am, one was called *Hamlin Family*, and consisted of Patrick and me; the other was called *Hamlins* and consisted of Patrick, his daughter and me.

At 11.06 I had been walking with the phone in my pocket. At the time, I didn't even know how to create a WhatsApp group. Full disclosure—I am pretty certain that Patrick when alive wouldn't have known either. We had both come to WhatsApp quite late and had only used it rarely. It was only since his illness that I had started to use it with any regularity.

I was completely bemused. There was absolutely no "rational" explanation for how this could have happened. I didn't immediately realize that his daughter would be notified about the *Hamlins* group, but of course she was, and she then sent me a WhatsApp asking why I had created a group with her father? I explained that no, I hadn't done so. I hadn't done it accidentally (how could one do that accidentally?); I hadn't done it while having a blackout; I hadn't done it subconsciously; I literally had not done it. Nor could it have happened through random jiggling in my pocket.

I then tried to create a WhatsApp group, to see how easy it was. It took me a little time to see how to do it, and I then tried to work out if it was possible to create two different groups both within one minute. Patrick's WhatsApp thread was right at the bottom of my list of contacts, because obviously it had not been used for six months, and I think that though a twelve-year-old with nimble fingers might just possibly have been able to create two groups within one minute, it would have taken great skill.

I could only attribute the two groups to Patrick. It seemed to me that Patrick had been giving his daughter a birthday present, showing her through the WhatsApp group that he was alive in spirit.

My son was sceptical. He spent ages trying to work out if my phone could have been hacked by someone intent on creating the two groups. In the end, he concluded that it would only have been possible if someone had had physical control of my phone—which of course hadn't happened.

I think that this episode illustrates Patrick's ingenuity. The two groups sent a wonderful message to his daughter and to me, a message of life in spirit and continuing love. By actually creating groups, with correct names, he did something which couldn't be explained away as a malfunction of the phone; he created something that I could look at and know was him saying, "Hi." It was extraordinary. It was brilliant.

The only thing which slightly baffles me is why he called the group with the three of us *Hamlins* and the group with just him and me *Hamlin Family*. I would have expected it to be the other way round. So that I can't explain. I suppose I can't explain the creation of the groups at all, other than as a miracle performed by Patrick—a miracle that finally and, I think irrefutably, proved to me that he still survived in spirit. 6 August 2019 was the day I knew for sure that all the apparent signs and coincidences that I and others had experienced had not been just random happenings, but had indeed been Patrick trying to contact me and to tell me that he still loved me and he was still consciously Patrick, albeit discarnate. This was the day when I realized that I no longer had to read books trying to prove the continuation of life after death, and I had read many, because now I knew for sure.

11

Patrick

In a way, I should not have been surprised by the persistence and ingenuity that Patrick had shown in his attempts to contact me. Patrick was an alpha male—a strong character always prepared to stand up for what was right. He could be an utterly charming guest or host, but on the other hand, he could be quite argumentative when he felt like it. I learnt early on not to kick him under the table when he was playing devil's advocate, because he was just as likely innocently to ask, "Why are you kicking me, darling?" as not. Why he had to bring up the deficiencies in American policing over a breakfast table with some twelve locals in Colorado, I know not. I know not, but it did not surprise me. When this sort of thing happened, I would rather wimpishly try to pour oil on troubled waters.

His attitude was possibly connected to the fact that he was a man of great integrity. He was straight, all the way through, and did not buy into the white-lies-for-social-ease scenario. He respected people enough to tell them the truth.

"We laugh a lot, don't we?" he would often exclaim as we laughed over the breakfast table at the latest instance of folly that we had heard on the radio. We shared the same sense of humour, and the same enjoyment in the idiosyncrasies of our friends and neighbours. Sometimes he would catch my eye at a gathering and I would have huge difficulty in keeping a straight face—we would know that we would have a good laugh about it later. I miss the laughter as much as anything.

As far as generosity is concerned, Patrick was the most generous man I have ever known. Not just in the always-first-to-buy-a-round type of generosity, but in a much more profound sense as well. Two different people came up to me at his funeral to say how he had helped them out with substantial sums of money when they were in financial difficulty, and this even though he always worried about money and feared not having enough. I think this was an abiding fear that went back to his childhood, but it never stopped him from sharing what he had. He was also generous with his time. He gave of his legal expertise unstintingly to friends and neighbours, and would spend hours helping someone in return for a mere thank you, or maybe a bottle of wine. But most importantly, he was generous in spirit. He would be aware of the foibles and pettiness of others, but he would be very forgiving. He never held a grudge and he accepted people as they were, feet of clay and all. He could understand what made people tick, and despite being a judge in criminal cases, he was rarely judgmental in his attitude.

He was also kind. One of the mediums I consulted said that he didn't have a malicious bone in his body, and that was true. And he was fearless. He had a scar on his chest to prove it. When he was 17, he encountered a burglar in his mother's house and chased after him up a dead end. Patrick ended up being knifed for his troubles. He could not understand why I was amazed that he had done that — in his eyes, anyone would have. He was a good man to have watching your back. When I was with him, I felt utterly safe, and I knew that he would rise to any challenge to protect me and look after me. When he lay dying, he worried about me and how I would manage without him. So if any spirit was going to literally move heaven and earth to send me comfort, it was Patrick. And he did. Big time.

12

Sand and Consciousness

That summer of 2019 I took Phoebe for a walk along the beach, and because it was nearly warm enough, I took off my socks and shoes to feel the damp sand with my feet. I was beginning to feel alive again, but I still needed lots of physical sensations to remind me that I was on this earth and part of the world.

In 2002, my then partner Rob had died of stomach cancer at the early age of 57. I had nursed him for the six months that he was ill, and he died at home in my arms. I was totally bereft, especially as my father had died just twelve days before. I remember that after the funeral some dear friends took me up to the north-west corner of Scotland, and we spent two weeks walking in the wild unspoilt landscape there. I used to strip off and jump naked into every tarn that we passed, even though it was September. The water was always icy cold and it would send shock waves through my whole system, and I could not stop myself screaming when I first went in, but I needed to feel a physical sensation—I needed to know that I was still a body, and not just the amorphous blob without boundaries that I seemed to have become in my grief.

This time around, I did not go to Scotland, but cold, wet sand on my feet was helpful, and again let me feel a physical boundary to my body. Of course, after the barefoot walk, I then had huge difficulty in wiping my feet clean before putting my socks back on, and the remaining gritty sand was quite uncomfortable. When I got home, I was pleased to be able to wash my feet, and put on new, sand-less socks.

It made me think about sand. A grain of sand is special. William Blake thought that heaven was in a grain of sand, and maybe he was right. I see a grain of sand as a fulcrum, the pivot on which balances the universe. It is said that there are more stars in the sky than there are grains of sand upon the earth, and yet, and equally astonishingly, there are also more atoms in one single grain of sand than there are grains of sand in this world. Although this might not be totally and utterly accurate, it is in a sufficiently close ballpark to make sense. This knowledge makes me realize how incredibly huge and how incredibly tiny are our surroundings, and how extraordinarily complex.

I wish I knew more about science, and understood what little I know. At school, I found physics boring—we just seemed to draw levers, and write up predictable experiments which always neatly ended with QED. And as for chemistry, I am sorry to say that I used to sit at the back and do my Latin homework. I ploughed through maths, but the numbers did not come alive for me, and I found it dry stuff. I was interested in people—in their lives, their stories, their languages. I loved history, geography, English, Latin, the humanities generally. Science left me cold. It was only after Patrick died that I wanted to understand life, science, consciousness, the universe. To start with, I read books about the afterlife, to see if it were real or not, but after 6 August 2019, I knew for sure that consciousness survived, and then I wanted to read about how that could possibly be. I started to read popular books on physics, and then quantum mechanics, and I became fascinated and confused in equal measure.

Quantum Effects

It seems to me that the more closely you looked at matter, the more it disappears. A grain of sand looks solid and stable, but inside it is a churning mass of subatomic particles which fly around empty space within their atoms. Energy seems to be the basis of matter and subatomic particles seem to be both wave and particle, and can pass through seemingly impenetrable barriers, as in quantum tunnelling, or can instantaneously affect another particle at the other side of the world—quantum entanglement. They can be in different potential positions at the same time, and are affected by observation, and even the intent of the observer. I find all this mind-boggling, and it shows how little we understand of the world, despite the predictability of our classical physics and our increasing use of quantum mechanics in all sorts of technologies. The fairly new research into quantum biology shows that the processes of life itself use and rely on quantum effects. Such diverse matters as photosynthesis and enzyme stimulation have been studied down to the quantum level, and no doubt more research will reveal more and more quantum effects supporting life as we know it. This means that we can no longer isolate the quantum world into a discrete, counter-intuitive box, and instead we must recognise that quantum effects inform the world we see around us, and throw into jeopardy all our preconceived notions as to how the world works.

The Mystery of Consciousness

This is reassuring to me when I think about consciousness.

Basically, there seem to be two main theories. Materialists say consciousness is created by the brain—though they can't say how or why. The "spirit" theory is that consciousness exists all around, and our brains are like radios that receive and transmit. This means that when the brain dies, the spirit, the consciousness, that was being transmitted is still there, just not functioning through a body. As the signs from Patrick became more and more irrefutable, I realized that his spirit still survived and was consciously Patrick. How else could I explain the WhatsApps and all the other manifestations of love and presence?

So now I think that consciousness is beyond matter—a belief rather like that of many Eastern religions. I don't understand the why or the wherefore, but I am absolutely sure that there is a self-aware consciousness that is Patrick who communicates with me, to my utter delight.

Scientist friends have laughed indulgently when I have said what I think, but the more I have read, the more I realize that there is a mass of evidence available to prove that life after death exists, that reincarnation happens, and that near-death experiences are not merely hallucinations caused by a malfunctioning brain. I find it quite extraordinary, and rather depressing, that so many academics and materialist scientists just refuse to look at the evidence that is available, and label all people interested in spiritualism as charlatans or idiots.

Of the many examples that I found persuasive, two come to mind. Both are described in a book by Leslie Kean called *Surviving Death*. The first is concerned with a near-death experience, where a patient described a shoe that she had seen on an outside window ledge of the hospital while out of her body. The shoe was later discovered where she had described it, even though it would have been impossible for her to have seen it beforehand from outside, or indeed from anywhere that she could have been. The second involves reincarnation, and is the well-documented case of little James Leininger, an American child who from the age of two knew about World War Two aeroplanes in uncanny detail. His memories of his previous life were recorded at the time and subsequently proved to match the life of an airman who had been shot down in the war. From the plethora of other cases, these two stand out as being quite inexplicable other than as evidence that the soul, the spirit, the energy, call it what you will, can leave the physical body, and return, or return in another body. Either way, consciousness can survive outside a body.

Time and Memory

This resonates with me, because of what I have experienced. The universe is mind-boggling, full stop. I try to understand that time is not the absolute it seems to me, but a part of a time-space continuum which is flexible and can go backwards as well as forwards. I imagine a spike, on which are piled up trillions of wafer thin papers, all of which represent moments in my life, but they are piled up vertically, rather than laid out horizontally, as if they are all informing my present. What I don't know is if the papers are already piled up beyond this particular moment as I write. There is a lot written about precognition nowadays. I am still sceptical, though I did experience it one time. It was in June 2019, and the village was holding a French Night in the Village Hall, with all proceeds going to a cancer charity in memory of Patrick. As usual, there was a raffle, and a strip of five tickets cost £5. I had done a lot of catering for the evening, and so I didn't feel obliged to buy more than one strip. A lot of people bought two or more. The strips were then torn up and the individual numbers put into a container, ready for the draw. I suddenly knew that I was going to win. It was a strange knowledge, but absolutely definite, and so I was not the least surprised when yes, my number was called out first. I was not even surprised when I won the third prize as well—not bad for a strip of five tickets.

Because I visualize time piled up, I imagine that memory is like a butterfly that flutters continually up and down the spike, landing lightly—or heavily—on different moments of time. My butterfly behaved strangely after Patrick died. On the one hand, it kept on returning to the row that we had had some months before Patrick was taken ill. During our time together, we obviously had disagreements, but we only ever had the one row, and that was short-lived and quickly resolved. I had forgotten all about it until after Patrick died when, in my grief, the butterfly of memory started to return to that slither of time, just as a tongue seeks out a hole in a tooth. I found it painful to remember and, oh, how I wished that I had not been cross and had not criticised him. I went over and over it again and again, torturing myself for having been angry. In my mind, a twenty minute row was elevated out of all proportion into a huge affair and this caused me tremendous guilt and regret. It took months to persuade the butterfly to move on.

On the other hand, the butterfly also went into deep hibernation and I could hardly remember anything else about our life together—it was all a complete blank in my mind. I had moments of panic, worrying that I had lost my memory permanently. Slowly, very slowly, more and more fragments of memory began to re-enter my consciousness, but it was a long process. Two years on, I can remember many good times that we had together, but it has taken until now for all the memories to come back. I wonder if the scary amnesia at the beginning, caused no doubt by shock, was also nature kindly preventing me from staring too deeply into the abyss.

13

Birds I

As I have said, one of the amazing mediums said that she saw Patrick surrounded by birds, and at the time, this didn't make any sense to me. I thought she'd got that wrong. She also said that she saw swallows, but again, this meant nothing. That was in April 2019.

One of Patrick's funny little habits was to salute magpies. He went through quite an elaborate ritual, making three figures of eight with his hand while intoning, "Good morning, Mr Magpie," three times for each sighting. This could make his driving quite dangerous, especially when there were several magpies, all of whom had to be saluted separately. When I teased him, Patrick used to point out that he had preserved me from all sorts of unspecified disasters by his salutations, and I think that some part of him really believed it.

Other than that, we were not really bird-aware. Yes, we had a nesting box high up on the house, and we were delighted when wagtails used it one year, but that was all. We did not feed the birds because we had two cats, one of whom was a hunter. Once both cats had died, then feeding became possible, and I remember one Christmas I found in my stocking some fat balls and maggots, together with the relevant feeders. I had great fun telling people that Father Christmas had brought me maggots! But other than sporadically noticing unusual birds in the garden, we were pretty oblivious to the amazing avian life surrounding us.

Then, in September 2018, just a month or so before Patrick became ill, we went on safari in Zambia. It was a very special holiday to celebrate my 65th birthday. To start with, we were only interested in the mammals—the antelope, the baboons, the lions, the elephants, the giraffes, the hyenas, the buffalo. We were thrilled to see—and learn—so much and we both loved watching all these animals in the wild. But towards the end of the ten day trip, we began to notice the birds. I think it was seeing the carmine bee-eater colony in the soft sandstone cliffs by the Luangwa River that entranced us, and then we began to listen to the calls and songs that surrounded us wherever we went. We watched vultures surrounding the remains of a dead antelope and we listened to the call of the hoopoe. We saw an African fish eagle. We discussed it one evening, and we both agreed that we were newly, and unexpectedly, fascinated by the birds and their stories. We both realized what we had been missing by not really being interested before, and we wanted to take note from then on.

Five months after Patrick died I drove down to the Dordogne to stay with my dear friends Anna and Ben. Fiona accompanied me on the journey, and we both felt a huge sense of relief when we finally arrived. Fiona has spent her whole—and very successful—working life in the travel industry, so it was surprising to find that she was hopeless when it came to map-reading, and somehow the satnav didn't seem to work very well in France. Anyway, we arrived to much hugging and kissing (this was, of course, 2019, before the pandemic) and also to much exclaiming and excitement about the swallows, who had been nesting in the outhouse roof above the washing machine and dishwasher. At the exact moment we arrived, the fledglings left the nest and started swooping around the courtyard with their parents. Their flight was fast and controlled—they were able to fly through the small doorway to their nest without braking. It seemed that there were swallows everywhere. At the time, I didn't remember what the medium had said, but it came back to me some months later.

In France, and then back in England, I found relief in sitting quietly outside and I gradually began to take note of the birds again. There was a strange croaking noise at dusk that I couldn't identify, and I wasn't even sure whether it came from a bird or an animal. One day, I was out walking in a nearby beech wood with Phoebe when I met an elderly couple and we began to talk. They said that they had just seen some ravens and when I was surprised they assured me that there were ravens around. I knew that ravens protected the Tower of London, but otherwise I associated them with Gothic romances and dark Scandinavian forests. Edgar Allan Poe had made them seem almost mythical to me. I was really astounded to learn that ravens lived in our quiet neighbourhood. The couple then said something about the croaking of ravens, and the penny dropped—I had been hearing ravens calling without realizing it. A mystery solved.

14

The Rizla Papers

The summer passed, and slowly the reservoir inside me became calmer and began to drain. I realized how wonderfully supportive all the children had been, and how they had kept me going through the dark months, when I was really unaware of anything outside my grief. I began to find the energy to interact with my grandchildren again, and of course, they were a source of delight. I remember staying with my daughter, and her four-year-old looking at the photograph of Grandpa Patrick by my bed. She asked me about it, and I explained that because he was in heaven, I could not be with him, so I liked to have a photograph of him instead. She said with all the confidence of a child, "But he can ring you!" Maybe she was right. Maybe that's what the WhatsApps were. It was a nice thought anyway. Then I had a week's holiday in the sun with one of my sons and his family, and I very much enjoyed our time together in new surroundings. I was slowly beginning to emerge into life.

In November 2019, three friends and I went to Cyprus for another week of sun. The holiday was a thank you to my friends, who had been so caring to Patrick and me during the dreadful days of his illness, and who had then helped me in all sorts of ways thereafter. We had a good week. The weather was hot and sunny, and we swam, ate, drank and generally relaxed. We also visited the painted churches for which Cyprus is so famous, and I lit a candle for Patrick in every church that I went into. The only disappointment, as far as I was concerned, was that the massive church in the middle of our village was always locked. We enquired in the shop nearby and we were told that the keyholder lived in the town and the church would not be opened until Sunday. We were going home on Saturday, so we had lost our chance of seeing inside. I so wanted to light another candle for Patrick, but it was obviously not to be.

On our last evening, Friday, 8 November 2019, we went out to a restaurant in the village as usual, and then walked home under the stars. Fiona was a smoker in those days (no longer), and when we arrived back, she looked for her Rizla papers to roll a cigarette. She was perplexed because she had left the papers on the big table in the living room—it was the table we sat round at mealtimes, and also it was large enough for us to leave our cameras, hats and other stuff on—but the papers were no longer there. She couldn't understand where they had gone; she was absolutely sure she had left them just there on the table. Jenny got up to help her in her search. The obvious thing was that the papers had fallen from the table, so Jenny looked on the floor, and also pulled out every chair to see if the papers had fallen on to a chair seat. No papers. Eventually we all searched throughout the villa for the wretched papers, but we didn't find them. Fiona had to go without her postprandial smoke.

The next morning, Fiona got up early to go to the shop as soon as it opened—she needed to buy more Rizla papers. We were all still in bed when she came rushing back, saying excitedly that the church was open for a service. So we leapt up and hurried to the church. We joined a fairly incomprehensible service, and then at the end, I was able to go and light a candle for Patrick. I was so pleased. I had really wanted to see the church interior and to confirm my presence and my love for Patrick with a candle.

We then walked back to our villa, and there, on one of the chairs that had been pulled out from under the table, and staring us all in the face, were… the missing Rizla papers.

I continue to be so impressed by Patrick's ingenuity. He worked out how to let us know that we could indeed get into the church. I was so grateful.

15

Illness

I have indeed much to be grateful about, and surprisingly, one of those things is my illness.

When I was first diagnosed with essential thrombocythemia, I was shocked and upset, but now, with perspective, I look on it as a blessing. It was in 1998 that I went to the doctor's because I just felt so tired and stressed. I thought it was probably because I was juggling a demanding job with raising three children as a single parent, but I decided that I would ask for help. The doctor did some blood tests, and rang me up late one evening to say that there was something wrong. Some time and examinations later, I was sitting in front of a specialist at Addenbrooke's Hospital in Cambridge and being given the diagnosis. I remember a few things about that meeting. The doctor told me that there could be complications in about ten years' time, and then he told me that I wouldn't make old bones. When I reacted with dismay, thinking about my children and myself as well, he told me quite impatiently that he didn't know why I was upset because he often had to tell people much worse things. Funnily enough, I didn't find this very consoling. Then I asked him what I could do to help myself, thinking about diet or exercise, and he replied, "Nothing."

The next day, I went to The Gambia with my friend Isobel. We had both been ill with coughs and colds throughout the winter, and we had booked a week at Easter to enjoy some sun. I can remember swimming up and down the pool, thinking, rather dramatically, that I was going to die. I was only 45 and I was going to die. I don't think that it can have been a very jolly holiday for Isobel.

When I arrived home, I arranged to take a second opinion,

and I saw a lovely avuncular man in London. He called me "my dear" and he assured me that I was unlikely to die of thrombocythemia—it would take so very long to get me that I was far more likely to die of something else first, and at a good old age. It is possible that the Cambridge doctor was scientifically more qualified than my London man, but in terms of empathy and patient psychology, the latter was streets ahead. I left feeling reassured, and thinking that I could control my health. And I did. I made sure to eat a healthy diet, and to get enough sleep and exercise.

Also, I decided to do lots of special things with the children, to build up their memory banks, just in case. So though I couldn't really afford it, I took all the children, and their friends, to Kalkan in Turkey for a villa holiday. My special friend Rob came too and we had a great time, despite being burgled on the second day and losing most of our cash. Rob was fit and healthy. He was 54. The memory bank was for my children and for him, but it turned out to be otherwise when he developed stomach cancer and died only three years later. So it was lucky that we went, but for an unanticipated reason.

When I moved down to live with Patrick in 2006, I started seeing Jenny, the bodywork healer, and she took on the job of keeping my bone marrow and the creeping fibrosis in check. Which she did and still does. It is now 22 years since the initial diagnosis and I am still well. I go for regular check-ups, and sometimes I see people who want to talk about the fact that I have a life-limiting disease, but I don't want to go there. I know that the doctors are caring and will prescribe medication or whatever as and when it becomes necessary, and that is reassuring. I also know that the doctors do not believe me when I say that the healing I am having is helping me. And that is fair enough. But I feel that the combination of happiness with Patrick, the energy work from Jenny and a generous dose of good luck have all been supporting me during this time. I know that other people have not had such good outcomes, and I feel very grateful for mine.

So why do I say that I see the illness as a blessing? Well, it hasn't yet become acute and it hasn't so far stopped me from doing anything, but it has made me very aware of my own mortality. Of course, I should have been aware anyway, but I wasn't. I was probably in denial. The illness brought me right up against the fact that I would die, and it could be sooner or it could be later—but it would definitely happen. And so I have learnt, through a combination of fear and common sense, not to rely on the future. I've realized that it is worth getting on with doing the things you want to do, or saying the things you want to say, rather than leaving stuff for another day. At the back of my mind I know that we have to live so that we can die without regrets, and we have to make sure that we've sorted things with our friends and family before the sun goes down. I think that all this has been an immensely valuable lesson, and one that I wouldn't have learnt without my troublesome bone marrow.

Of course, Patrick's illness was anything but a blessing. I still don't understand why he got bile duct cancer, and why he had to die at the comparatively young age of 71, when he was still so needed and loved here on earth. The only thing I can hold on to is that he is still conscious as a spirit, and he must be, because of the extraordinary signs that he has sent me since he died.

16

Feathers

Throughout this time, I kept finding feathers in extraordinary places. The literature is full of people interpreting feathers as signs, and I was always reluctant to follow suit, because you often see feathers as you go through your day, and they are a natural result of birds moulting, or being attacked or whatever. But sometimes I would find feathers in seemingly impossible places, and as the more obvious signs caused me to change my attitude, so I became more open to these soft messages too.

One morning in June 2019, at the time when I was receiving the WhatsApp messages, I found a white feather stuck with some force into my jumper, which was lying on the chaise longue in my bedroom. I had taken the jumper off the night before and left it there, in my usual, rather untidy way. My bedroom window had been open, although the curtains were drawn, but the way the feather's small quill was so deeply plunged into the jumper, while the feather itself stood proudly erect, was most unusual. It had not just fallen on to the jumper—it had been poked into it. I could not see how that had happened accidentally, or naturally.

A couple of months later, about six months after Patrick had died, I was on the train going home from my son's. A woman was sitting across the table from me, and because I had Phoebe with me, we started to chat. Spaniels are great icebreakers, and Phoebe was behaving remarkably well, for once. (Actually, that's unfair. She is always very good on trains, which is impressive because she had rarely been on one before Patrick died.) Anyway, the woman and I got to talking, and we discovered that we were both widows. We talked some more, and something the woman said made me feel emboldened to ask if she had received any signs after her husband had died. I asked it quite casually, and was gratified when she immediately launched into a long story about what had happened to her. She then asked me if I had had any signs. I did not tell her about the WhatsApps, because I did not want to seem quite mad, but I told her about some feathers. She interrupted me to say, "Look!" As I had been talking, a feather had floated down on to the book in front of me. Neither of us could see any possible source for this feather. The windows were of course all hermetically sealed, and no other passenger had been walking past at the time. I picked it up and put it in my notebook.

Two days later, when I went down in the morning, I found a large feather in the kitchen. All the windows and doors had been shut and I could find no rational explanation as to how the feather could have got there overnight.

Another feather appeared, as if it were from nowhere, when I was seeing Maria. After the strange WhatsApps from Maria's phone earlier in the year, I contacted her again in the autumn of 2019, to ask if we could meet once more. On 29 October, as we were messaging each other to fix a date, she sent me an extraordinary video of rays of light which lit up her whole sitting room. She wrote:

Look at their beautiful rays that has just happened as we are texting it's not sunlight as it's bloody miserable outside I've just tried to record it but I don't think it's letting me send it I hope it does it just lit up the whole room xx

OK I'm really hoping that you get the video it was beautiful I've not seen anything like that before in my living room.

She went on to write:

I feel really honoured to have these wonderful things happen when we talk xx

Two strange things happened during the reading that we subsequently had. We were in Maria's very minimalist dining room, which had no soft furnishings at all. The windows and door were closed. A feather suddenly floated down on to my shoulder. It seemed to appear out of nowhere, and there was no apparent source for a feather anywhere in the room. The second thing was that the ornamental clock, which had stopped months ago, suddenly started ticking, though the hands didn't move. Apparently it continued to tick for three or four hours after I had gone, and then stopped again.

Feathers continued to appear in unlikely places, and though perhaps the individual occurrences would not impress a sceptic, I accepted each one with gratitude. I am receiving, or seeing, fewer feathers now, but every so often a feather still reveals itself in an unlikely place, and usually after I have been thinking about Patrick, and missing him.

17

Early 2020 and a New Start

2020, the year of perfect vision, dawned, and it was time to start building a new life out of the rubble. Patrick had been dead for nearly a year, and I had come to understand that I had to make the best of my remaining time on this earth, and not become submerged in what-might-have-been. I had successfully avoided Christmas, which I had been dreading, by going on a singles holiday to Morocco, and though I had had my tearful moments, I also found myself enjoying the scenery of the Atlas Mountains and, in short bursts, the company of others. So Morocco was a good choice, and I told the children that we would have a big family Christmas in 2020, by which time I hoped to be in a better place. The best laid plans...

I decided to take some steps to alleviate my loneliness. I hated being in the house by myself—it was too quiet and empty—so I sorted out a bedroom, and posted it on spareroom.com, to find a lodger. I was unhappy about the first applicant, who complained that the wardrobe (previously mine) was too small for all her clothes, and this even though she was only looking for temporary accommodation for work, and would be going home at weekends. I could not envisage my happily sharing a kitchen with her. But then I struck lucky. A young man in his early twenties responded to my posting and I was so pleased when he liked the room, and asked to take it. Two weeks later, he came to lodge with me. We soon began to take it in turns to cook for each other and then eat together, in a lovely companionable way. I was thrilled with how it was turning out. It was such a pleasure to share the house again. An added bonus was that my lodger liked dogs and took Phoebe for long walks—I had found it quite onerous to be the sole provider of exercise for a very energetic spaniel. My first proactive step into the future was a resounding success.

I also realized that it was time to return to my pottery studio. I had not been inside it since Patrick had died; the bereavement had drained me of any creative energy. I still found it hard to go in, because Patrick had been such an interested and helpful supporter of my endeavours, and had regularly popped in when I was working, to see how I was getting on, and to bring me a cup of tea. So I had the idea of giving lessons to friends. It worked brilliantly for me. I had company in the studio, and I began to get used to being there without Patrick. I felt that it was a case of onwards and upwards, and I felt rather proud of myself for beginning to build the structure of a new life.

The First Anniversary and Chinese Food

February of course brought with it the first anniversary of Patrick's death. To mark the occasion, his children and I decided to meet for a Chinese meal in London. Patrick had always loved Chinese food and he liked nothing better than to go to Chinatown for authentic food. So remembering Patrick in a good Chinese restaurant was fitting and appropriate. We met up, we toasted him and we reminisced. I can remember laughing at some of the outrageous stories and feeling close to tears at the same time. Patrick had always had a fund of good stories. One concerned a cheap Chinese restaurant in Liverpool, or possibly Birmingham, that he went to when he was a young barrister. The place was family-run. The food was terrible. The family themselves also realized this, because when they wanted to eat, they sent out for takeaway and then sat round a table at the back of the room eating the food that had been brought in from elsewhere. Patrick delighted in the absurdity of it.

Another of Patrick's stories concerned a menu which was in Chinese with the English translations by the side. At the end of the menu were two or three Chinese dishes which did not carry any translation. Patrick of course asked what they were. The waiter replied that they were not for him but only for Chinese people. This only encouraged Patrick to insist. He and the waiter had a more and more heated discussion, until eventually the waiter said triumphantly, "They are a pig's entrails" — dramatic pause — "and the entrails have not been cleaned!" (Whether this was true, I know not.) Patrick was defeated and he knew it. He weakly said, "Oh, right, um, okay, I will have the chow mein please."

We remembered these and other stories. We remembered how Patrick loved going to Chinese supermarkets and buying all sorts of unidentifiable ingredients. He would also buy monosodium glutamate, which I disapproved of. As I tended to do most of the cooking, these strange packets and the flavour enhancer would linger in the larder or at the bottom of the freezer for years. Only the other day, I found some strange-looking dumplings hiding behind a frozen leg of lamb.

It was a good way to mark the anniversary. Patrick had loved his children and was immensely proud of them. We all missed him tremendously, but we laughed too, and that was good.

18

Lockdown

And then the tragedy of COVID struck, and we had lockdown. My lovely lodger lost his job and went home to Scotland. I had to stop giving my pottery lessons, and I felt as though the small, tentative steps I had taken to reconstruct my life had been destroyed in a single blow. I was bitterly disappointed and for a week or two thought that I was back to square one. But actually, I was in a much stronger place than I had been some months previously, and I did know now that I would be able to rebuild my life when lockdown was over. Through necessity, I had to live in the house by myself, and I gradually got used to it and began to feel less lonely. I still felt Patrick's absence intensely, but I found that I had some energy now to think about other things, such as the world around me, as well. I felt huge empathy for all the suffering and grief that was accompanying the pandemic. The thought of all that bereavement was horrendous and, in particular, that such bereavement would be taking place in isolation.

While others were grieving, or working heroically, or suffering emotionally or financially under the strict terms of lockdown, I was lucky. My daughter, the mother of three girls aged two, five, and eight, asked for help with home-schooling, and so we set up a Zoom session every weekday morning. For me, it was the most wonderful therapy—although I suspect the girls would describe it somewhat differently. I almost felt closer to the children than ever, because we interacted every day. I loved the structure, and I loved the fun of watching the girls develop.

With the lengthening days I started to spend hours in the summerhouse again and my interest in the birds—and nature generally—continued to grow. And meanwhile, there was also renewed activity on the WhatsApp front, which of course thrilled me.

19

Later WhatsApps

After our meeting in October, I had not had any further contact with Maria until January 2020, when a WhatsApp arrived from her phone to mine:

Dfjk8888888upliftyllimafnilmah

And no, Maria said she had not sent it.

Then, on 9 April 2020, Maundy Thursday and deep in lockdown, Patrick sent me more WhatsApps from Maria's phone. It was late at night and, as usual, Maria had no idea. Again, Sri Lanka was mentioned. This is how it went:

"::34srlkx21
78888
Hamlinfamywataapp
Sri Lanka 170219.
Dddghrty
Semillionciris

The first two lines meant nothing to me. The reference to the *Hamlin Family* WhatsApp was significant. This was one of the groups that had been created while the phone was in my pocket in August 2019. In February 2020, I had received notification that Patrick had left that group and the second group, called *Hamlins*. I was quite upset at the time, but then research revealed that WhatsApp automatically takes people out of groups if they have not shown any activity for over six months.

The mention of Sri Lanka was intriguing because that had come up in a previous WhatsApp, and the date, 17 02 19 was the date when Patrick had been alive but in a coma. I thought the last line looked like *send a million kisses,* which I gladly accepted. The next day, this arrived:

170219]]]{^+,| | | | | | | | | | | | | | | | | | | | \ _]{{{]| \ |>€%}%$!$#{\]|, $!$#{\]|,~~~<<<<<<~~<<<<<<<<<<<<<<<<<<<<<<<<<<{#%?*

It obviously didn't make much sense, apart from the date.

I no longer doubted Maria because I knew that Patrick could indeed manipulate WhatsApp. So when the following came, on 29 April 2020, again apparently from Maria's phone, but without her knowledge, I was pleased to receive it.

*..,:/.,;)££;/::3:,.,(
I :/lo6(!youdarli:(myha00iestYear/aaa/-@&" Day*

I interpreted that as I love you darling, my happiest year and day.

The next event was on 1 May 2020 when I received a notification that Maria's phone had created a new WhatsApp group called *Hamlin Family* and consisting of her and me. When I asked her about it, she denied all knowledge, but then I got this WhatsApp from her:

My daughter has just shown me in my notifications there is a message from Hamlin family saying I created a group .it wasn't me I wonder why Patrick didn't just communicate through are regular wats app clearly he wants us to use Hamlin family else why would he of done that xx

I think it was ingenious of him. He could no longer use his old phone as part of a WhatsApp group, but he had reinstated the group that he had created with me the previous August. He was resourceful as ever.

On 1 June 2020 a message came to the new *Hamlin Family* group. It said:

/://(1435darlingsseeetryvdimgonettyuioHamlinnnhjfam

I could see a *darling* and *trying go you Hamlin Family* in that, as if Patrick were saying that he was trying to contact me via the *Hamlin Family* WhatsApp.

20

Flying Books

Although my yearning for Patrick was, with the passage of time, less intense, I still felt very alone and the lockdown could also be difficult to navigate. I had last had a reading with a medium, Maria, at the beginning of November, and six months later, feeling down, I booked a skype call with another medium. We spoke on 5 May 2020. She was good, and I felt very heartened by her words. One point was, she said that Patrick told me to pay attention to the birds. That inspired me to look for the binoculars so I could take them up to the summerhouse. I had given Patrick a good pair of field binoculars for his birthday shortly before we went on safari, and so I knew there were some in the house, but though I searched, I couldn't find them anywhere.

Two nights later, in the early hours of 7 May, I was lying in bed, unable to sleep and chatting to Patrick in my head, when suddenly there was an almighty thump outside my open bedroom door, on the half landing. I was terrified. I lay frozen for maybe a minute, listening intently, but could hear nothing. Oh for a strong and brave husband to nudge. But there wasn't one, so I nervously reached out to turn on the light, and waited—again nothing. Summoning my courage, I slipped out of bed, put on my nightdress for some flimsy protection, and cautiously tiptoed out into the landing. A book was lying open and face down on the carpet. There is a bookcase on the far wall, and *Started Early, Took My Dog* by Kate Atkinson had flown out from an upper shelf on to the floor. No one else was in the house and there was no draught or any other reasonable explanation as to how or why the book had precipitated itself off the shelf and on to the floor with such force. When I knelt down to pick it up, I saw the binoculars that I had been searching for—they were tucked in on a low shelf. I could only think that it was dear Patrick, supporting my interest in birds.

Some four months later, I was again awake in the small hours. This time, it was 4am, and I was sitting up in bed drinking a cup of tea. As usual, I was missing Patrick, and, very specifically, I was wondering why he had had to leave me. Suddenly, there was an almighty crash on the half landing. This time, I was not so scared, and anyway, I already had the light on, to drink my tea. So, quite calmly in the circumstances, I got up and went to see what had happened. Again, there was a book that had fallen with great force on to the carpet. This time it was *A Perfect Spy* by John le Carré. Again, no one else was in the house, and there was no draught or rational explanation. I felt that Patrick was showing me that he hadn't left me but was still around.

21

Birds II

During the summer of 2020, while COVID continued to wreak its destruction, I continued to observe and learn about nature. I put up a bird feeder near the summerhouse, and sat quietly for hours on end, still grieving but finding solace in watching the birds, and other animals and reptiles, come and go. My life was so much richer now that I noticed this extraordinary life around me. I heard a cuckoo calling and thought that he had just flown in all the way from Africa—a long journey as I knew because I had done it by plane. I was lost in awe. Then for several weeks I had huge pleasure in observing blue tits which were nesting in a crevice in the summerhouse roof. The parents worked tirelessly feeding their young, and I watched with joy in my heart as the fledglings learnt to fly.

Two buzzards patrolled the large pasture bowl that I looked out on. Their lonely cry was often the backdrop to my musings, and they provided much theatre. One day, there was a kerfuffle in the copse just beside me, and I watched a buzzard flying past with a baby rabbit in its talons. Several times I watched rooks— or crows?—noisily mob a buzzard and send it on its way. (I use the country way to tell the difference between a rook and a crow: *if you see a crow with its friends, it's a rook, and if you see a rook by itself, it's a crow.* I am not sure how that squares with the large mixed corvid roosts in the trees round about, and maybe the colour of the beak is a more accurate indicator, but that can be tricky to spot, and my way is easier.) During the summer, I watched two parent buzzards with their little one, teaching it to surf the thermals and how to hunt. They would fly with the little one between them and it was a delight to see the good parenting.

Nature suddenly took centre stage in all the conversations about how to survive lockdown, and I felt very lucky to have a garden and countryside around me, so I could immerse myself in nature all day and every day. And yes, it was very, very healing. Lockdown was a nightmare for many, if not most, people, but to me it brought an unexpected benefit. It gave me the space and the time just to be, without any pressure to socialize, or to do or achieve anything. I had the opportunity to heal slowly and quietly in my own time.

22

The Missing Playing Card

On 7 October 2020, I was playing bridge with three friends in my dining room.

You use two packs of cards when you play bridge, one alternating with the other. We had a red pack and a blue pack that day, both fairly new. We played with the red pack first and then the blue. So Jane, whose turn it was, dealt the red pack again for the third hand, and found that she was a card short. It sometimes happens that a dealer deals two cards at once by mistake, or loses track and deals out of sequence, so it was not particularly surprising that she was a card short, and we all counted the cards that we had been dealt, to see who had an extra card. But no one had; we all had the requisite 13 cards, other than Jane who only had 12. That seemed a bit odd, but we assumed that somehow a card must have fallen on to the floor, so we started to hunt for it. The card was nowhere to be found. We became more and more determined to find it: we stood up and checked our seats, we scoured the room. There was no card to be seen. This was extraordinary, because we knew that the pack had been complete for the previous hand.

Someone suggested that we should see which card it was. Sarah, who knew about all the strange signs I had received, said, "I bet it's a heart." And it was, the nine of hearts. They asked me if the nine was significant in any way, but I said no. I would have understood an ace of hearts, or a queen of hearts, but a nine seemed totally random. Still, it was all so peculiar, and I thought that it must be Patrick who had somehow dematerialised the card. I felt a warm glow and very loved.

We found a new pack of cards and carried on playing.

When I told a friend about it, she was really excited that it was the nine. She does tarot, which neither Patrick nor I had ever done or known about. She said that the nine of cups, the tarot equivalent, was a wonderful card. It represented very deep love, and it was also called the gypsy card or the wish card because it would give you what you wish for. She explained that while the three of cups suggested marriage, the couple and the priest, the nine represented three times the love found in a marriage. She felt that it was the best possible card to be a sign for me. I was delighted and also found it really funny that Patrick, who would have had no truck with tarot while alive, had somehow learned about its meaning while in spirit.

Since then, I have continued to look for the card, and every so often, I count the cards in the red pack, but the nine of hearts is still missing.

23

Lights

After Karen reported the strange case of her bedside lights, shortly after Patrick died, I occasionally found lights unexpectedly switched on. But I hesitated to ascribe this to Patrick, because there was always the chance that I had left a light on absent-mindedly, or unthinkingly turned one on. When I found the bedside lights on in the so-called ironing room, a spare bedroom that contains the ironing board, I was taken aback, because I had not been into the room for quite some time, but I did not take it as a sign. I could not remember exactly when I had last been there, and so I could not be sure that I hadn't switched on the lights then. (In retrospect, I am pretty certain it was a sign. The door was open to the landing, so I would surely have noticed if lights been on in the room for days beforehand.)

During the autumn of 2020, however, there were two occasions when I felt totally certain that Patrick was indeed sending me signs via the lights. No doubt he was feeling rather frustrated that I had not noticed or had ignored his previous attempts in that regard.

On Thursday, 29 October, I was in the sitting room. It was about 7pm, and I had lit the fire and turned on the lamps, which gave a warm and comforting glow to the room. I had not turned on the rather harsh ceiling downlights. I glanced idly at the coffee table, where a book I had just bought, *Those who are Loved* by Victoria Hislop, was atop the pile of reading that had accumulated there. I gave myself a mental hug and thought, "Well, yes, I am loved by Patrick" — and immediately, the ceiling lights came on. It was instantaneous. There was absolutely no possible "normal" explanation for what had happened. I was at some distance from the switch, and no one else was in the house. It was definitely a sign. Patrick was agreeing that he loved me. I felt... happy.

Fast forward to December, and I was driving home from a walk with Anna. It was a grey day and I was feeling a little down. All my plans and preparations for a cheerful family Christmas were suddenly redundant because my family in London would no longer be allowed to come as the coronavirus was still wreaking havoc, especially in the large cities. Many people were still dying, and I felt rather guilty for feeling despondent, when it was only Christmas that had been cancelled but, even so, I was bitterly disappointed. So I spoke to Patrick as I drove, and I asked him for another sign.

The next morning, the sign arrived. The dining room is off the kitchen, and there are glass double doors between the two rooms, so I always see into the dining room when I am going about my daily chores. Old-fashioned bookshelves line two of the dining room walls, and they have prominent brass lights arching over the fronts. I never turn these library lights on — they are decorative rather than functional. Their switch is hidden round the side of one of the bookshelves, away from the usual light switches. So when I glanced into the dining room and saw the library lights on, I knew that it must be a sign. I thanked Patrick in spirit.

24

Happiness

Maybe now is the time to talk about happiness. It may seem strange to talk about happiness in a book on bereavement, but of course it is the absence of happiness that is one of the burdens of grief. I can remember seeing a counsellor after Rob died. I was distraught because his death had been long and painful, and my father had died just a few days before. Life seemed bleak. I felt totally alone in the world, which of course was not true, because I had my children and my friends, but the two deaths within twelve days of each other had heightened a feeling of abandonment which went back to my childhood. I wept and told the counsellor that I feared I would never be happy again. I will always remember her reply. She said, "You will be happy again, but not for a while yet. It will take time." She was prescient. Little did I know that the happiest years of my life were yet to come. I met Patrick three years later, and embarked on a period of total happiness.

During my difficult times, I always tried to be positive, and see my glass as half full, not half empty. I have a friend who persists in seeing everything through a glass half-empty prism. Her marriage is not particularly affectionate, but she has other things in her life which are good, and by concentrating on the negative stuff, she is just permanently miserable. It is such a waste. I have always believed in the power of positive thinking, and it can make a huge difference but, even so, it does not seem to be quite enough to bring happiness.

The problem is, I do not think that happiness is a freestanding emotion, like fear or grief, love or joy, or even enthusiasm. Instead, I think that happiness rides on top of and depends on other independent emotions, in a sort of commensal relationship. So you cannot chase happiness as an end in itself—if you do, it proves elusive, like a will-o'-the-wisp. But if you seek fulfilment in your job or family or whatever, or if you seek joy in your garden, or contentment in your daily life, then happiness unexpectedly grows and envelops you.

In the most profound grief, happiness is a total irrelevance. All that matters is what is not there. Everything is black. But during the second year after Patrick died, I began to involve myself in life again, and surreptitiously happiness crept up and surprised me when I was busy doing or thinking about something else. To start with, the moments were fleeting and I almost felt guilty for feeling happy, but gradually the moments grew longer and I felt more comfortable with the feeling. Now, two years on, I would not claim to be happy all the time, nor would I claim that I am never unhappy, but I am more or less reconciled to what has happened, and I enjoy my life despite the loss of Patrick and despite the restraints of a continuing lockdown. I have learnt that happiness can return in the fullness of time even after the most devastating bereavement.

25

The Second Anniversary

February 2021 arrived with two milestones looming. The previous year, I had been so overwhelmed by the enormity of the anniversary of Patrick's death that I had not noticed Valentine's Day. This year was different, and I was dreading the day because Patrick and I had always celebrated it. We would give each other cards and he would give me flowers. We had then always gone out somewhere special for dinner. Funnily enough, the most romantic Valentine's dinner we ever had was the year that a dreadful storm toppled trees throughout the South West and cut off the electricity to thousands of houses, including ours. Two large old trees in the garden opposite were uprooted in the wind, and the only reason they did not crash into our house was that they were held back by a thin power line. The fire brigade came and told us that we had to evacuate the house until the trees could be safely taken down. Our plan to go further afield was obviously thwarted by the weather, and we ended up taking refuge in the pub, which had no electricity, but lots of candles, a blazing wood fire and, luckily, a Calor gas cooking range. Just a few neighbours who could walk to the pub also arrived, and we spent the evening listening to the wind and feeling cosy and companionable in the stricken bar. There is nothing like an emergency to bring people together. Eventually, at midnight, a team from the electricity board arrived and they skilfully brought down the trees under the glare of their lights. Patrick in particular was relieved that our house was saved—I had been annoyingly unworried—and we were able to go home to bed.

So this Valentine's Day, I felt lonely. It was as it was, and I tried to deal with it by remembering past happiness. I also had the consolation, deep inside, of knowing that I was still loved by the spirit of my husband.

Then, shortly after, came the second anniversary of Patrick's death. This year I could not meet up with his children for a Chinese meal, because of lockdown. That in itself was disappointing. And then I found that the anniversary was far more painful than I had expected. I had told the children beforehand that it would be okay, and I thought it would, because I remembered and missed Patrick every day anyway, and so the anniversary would be no different. I was wrong. I found myself reliving in vivid technicolour the whole horrendous 48 hours: Patrick lapsing into a coma and then fighting and struggling for breath for two long days. The children and I had kept him company throughout, and the memory was like a nightmare. I felt relieved when the 18th dawned, because that was the day when Patrick was released.

Two New WhatsApp Groups

The first thing that happened on the actual anniversary involved a new WhatsApp group. In the morning, I received a notification that Maria had created a group on her phone consisting of her and me, called simply 1. Unsurprisingly, Maria had not done it, and she had thought it must have been me. None of this seemed strange to me. By now, I knew that Patrick could manipulate WhatsApp, and that the creation of a group was his ingenious way of sending me a message. Later on that afternoon, he created yet another group on Maria's phone, this time called A. I do not know why the groups were given such brief names, when the groups from earlier had been given full names, but it did not matter to me. I knew that Patrick was aware that it was the anniversary of his death, and that he was okay.

It was what happened next that was truly remarkable, but I need to backtrack to explain the context.

BulliesOut

After Patrick died, I struggled to make sense of his senseless death. He had been so strong and so vigorous, and he still had so much to give. It seemed absurd that he had contracted cancer and died. I felt totally floored by the randomness of it all. Eventually, I realized that the only way I could make some sort of sense of his death was by trying to create something positive out of the disaster. I decided that I would set up a charity in Patrick's memory, as so many other bereaved people have done. However, the more I looked into it, the more I realized how complicated all the administration would be, and how I did not have enough money to make the charity viable long-term. So instead, I decided to find an existing charity with which I could collaborate.

Patrick had supported various charities while he was alive, but none of them especially spoke to me. I then had a thought. Patrick had lived in Hong Kong with his parents as a child and had attended the Peak School, where he had been very happy and had flourished. But then, a month after his eighth birthday, he was sent off to England, to board at a school in the North West. At the time, in the 1950s, this school was a cruel place, with a sadistic sociopath for a headmaster and rampant bullying throughout. Patrick arrived as an enthusiastic and innocent newcomer, and was immediately a target. His mother refused to believe his stories, and would not let him change school. It is to his immense credit that he survived and grew into a glorious oak tree rather than a stunted bush. Many children would have been scarred for life. I realized that if I did something about bullying, then I could create something good out of the viciousness of 60 years ago, and out of Patrick's untimely death.

I did not want a charity that paid its managers fat salaries. Rather, I wanted a small but effective charity—one that punched above its weight, and one where my contribution would make a real difference.

After a lot of research, I decided to work with BulliesOut, a charity started by Linda James and doing excellent work in the field. We put together a plan, whereby for five years I would support programmes for primary age pupils in memory of Patrick. I felt really pleased with the whole project.

So that is the background. Now to return to the second anniversary of Patrick's death. I contacted Maria again, when the second WhatsApp group came through, and this time, she replied that she did not know about it because she had taken her daughter to the dentist, and had not looked at her phone for some time. She added that her Safari (a web browser) had been playing up all day and had kept on opening up on "some charity's page" or on some newspaper report. She was unimpressed and frustrated.

I asked her to send me the pages that kept on showing up and the first one was a page—the merchandising page—from BulliesOut. I had never mentioned BulliesOut, or indeed any charity, to Maria. Though she features quite regularly in this account, I had only seen her twice over the last two years, and I was only in touch with her when Patrick seemed to be using her as a portal and when strange things were happening with WhatsApps. I was bowled over. I was also thrilled, because I took it that Patrick knew about the support project in his name, and endorsed it.

As for the other page that kept turning up uninvited on Maria's Internet, I felt there was a message there too. The story was about a teenager from Sri Lanka who was living in The Netherlands, and who committed suicide after being badly bullied at his school. I was struck by the Sri Lankan aspect— three times in the WhatsApps, Sri Lanka has been mentioned, and I have no idea why. We had never had any plans to visit the country and Patrick had no connection to it. But I was also struck by the fact that the child was a teenager, and I decided to extend the remit of the support project to secondary school pupils as well. I thought that that must have been Patrick's purpose in highlighting the report.

26

Ducks in a Row

Before and around the time of the second anniversary, I found that more and more memories of our life together came flooding back. And I realized that I could think about our relationship with not exactly a dispassionate approach, but a more analytical frame of mind than ever before. I could see why we had been attracted to each other. We had similar backgrounds, and we shared the same values. We understood each other. It is a wonderful feeling to know that your partner "gets" you; it means that you don't have to explain and you feel validated and integrated despite your complexity. We enjoyed the same things and we had similar goals.

That is not to say that we were the same, because we emphatically were not. And indeed, it would be very boring to live with someone who was in effect your clone. Patrick was quite ordered. He always used to say that, before arguing a case, the important thing was to get all your ducks in a row. Once he had his ducks in a row, he was ready to take on the world. I, on the other hand, was more disorganized and less careful with my ducks. So he brought stability and I brought a certain anarchy to our life together.

I remember when we were planning a homeward journey after a holiday in San Sebastián in northern Spain. Our idea was to spend one night in the Dordogne, and then the second night further north, nearer to Cherbourg, the ferry port from which we were going to sail. At the time, we were drinking Tour de Chollet wine, and we knew the vineyard ran a B&B. I remembered from school that Chollet was in the Loire Valley, so it seemed a great idea to book in and I did. The night before we travelled back, Patrick went on to the Internet to plan the route, and discovered to his horror that Tour de Chollet was not in the Loire but in the Dordogne, south of where we were going to stay. Who knew that the Cholet in the Loire was spelt differently? Well, unfortunately, I didn't. The B&B had been very kind, and had agreed to take Phoebe despite their general rule of no pets, and so we did not feel able to cancel at such short notice. We left our first stay in the Dordogne on the Sunday and reluctantly backtracked south. On the Monday morning, we had to set the alarm for 4.30am so as to get to the ferry in time. Luckily, Patrick thought it was very funny, and we added the episode to our long history of misadventures that were due to those wretched ducks not being in a row.

Yes, we were different, and so we obviously had some different ideas. Most of our disagreements we managed to resolve, but not all. I liked to leave clearing up after a supper party until the morning; Patrick liked to clear up before going to bed. We never really found a perfect solution to that one. Likewise, I never managed to stop him just leaving his shoes in the middle of the kitchen floor. I would occasionally try nagging, but that was useless. I would cry "ouch" and hop around, pretending to have stubbed my toe, but that had no effect either. He would just laugh. Remembering these irritations, which were part of the rhythm and routine of our life together, I realized that I missed the annoyances as much as I missed anything. Any relationship is multifaceted, and everything goes into the mix. I felt that the two of us together were greater than the sum of our parts, and that was both wonderful and also devastating when it was no more. No wonder bereavement is so painful—the survivor loses not only a loved one, but also the jointly-created structure of intertwined lives. It leaves the one left behind feeling incomplete, and only now, two years on, am I starting to feel whole again.

27

Epilogue

As I write this epilogue in March 2021, a month after the second anniversary of Patrick's death, time is playing its strange tricks. On the one hand, I can hardly believe that it is two long years since I last held Patrick in my arms, since I last spoke to him and heard his voice, since we last laughed and joked and cared for each other in a cocoon of intimacy and love. On the other hand, the two years have passed at a snail's pace, and often seemed interminable. February 2019 seems just a blink away, and a lifetime away, both feelings existing together in some strange conjunction in my mind.

But within my sadness, there is also joy. Last October, we toasted Patrick at my younger son's wedding. It was a very happy occasion, despite the COVID restrictions, and I could imagine Patrick saying, "At last!" He had thoroughly approved of the match, and had been impatient for my son to get a move on. Then in January his daughter gave birth to a baby boy, who looks like Patrick—he definitely has the same ears—and whose middle name is Patrick.

And so Patrick's genes continue, and though this little baby will never know his grandfather, he will be told lots of stories about him, and the loving way that Patrick brought up his children will inform how his daughter brings up this little one and his brother. Knowing and loving Patrick as I did also informs my behaviour. I still stop to think, "What would Patrick do?" when I am faced with a difficult situation, and I still want to make him proud of me. His influence lives on. I am sure his influence lives on with other people as well, not only with his family but with friends, acquaintances, and even strangers. Just as a small tossed pebble creates ever-increasing ripples in a pool, so little acts of kindness or generosity end up having extraordinarily widespread effects, and, who knows?, maybe the ripples of Patrick's life are still having effects all over the world. I like to think so.

A medium told me, quite early on, that Patrick was saying he hadn't realized how important love was. I always knew that I loved Patrick from the depth of my heart, but I didn't know how powerful love was, and how it could bring messages and hope from the afterlife. I didn't even know there was an afterlife, for goodness' sake. The sheer number of signs and messages that I have received, and the extraordinary WhatsApp groups in particular, have proved to me that spirit survives, and so does love. Apart from the first signs received by my friends, which at the time I was reluctant to acknowledge, but which slowly began to erode my resistance to belief in the "paranormal", as I saw it, I have not included in this book the many subsequent signs that friends, in particular Jenny, have received. I have restricted myself to chronicling my direct experiences, experiences which I now cannot doubt. That confidence means that I still feel loved by Patrick, and it is a huge comfort to me at all times.

His loss is like a heavy stone within my being. Its sharp edges have been worn away with time, and so now it is rounded and is no longer acutely painful. Sometimes, it is cushioned by positive feelings of love, and other times, it is hard and unyielding and seems a bitter weight to carry. A bitter weight, but one I would not be without, because it also carries my memories of Patrick and my past happiness. And it will accompany me as I walk into my future happiness.

I hope that this account will give readers the reassurance that, with time, grief does soften, and that glimmers of light will appear, and will gradually grow stronger and brighter.

I also hope that, reading this, people will gain the confidence to recognise and accept signs and messages that they receive from their loved ones. I want people to know that consciousness, spirit, the soul, call it what you will, survives bodily death, because it is such a wonderful solace. This is not tied up with any religion. It just is as it is. This knowledge has totally changed my view of life and the world, and it has given me an inner security that I cherish. I wish the same for anyone who is bereaved.

The End

Time Line

16 February 2019	Patrick loses consciousness
18 February 2019	Patrick dies
23 February 2019	Jenny sees flame
6 March 2019	Jenny hears *I Want You to Want Me* on station Tannoy
18 March 2019	White feathers
1 April 2019	Medium on phone says Patrick died 16th February
6 April 2019	Karen finds bedside lights on
3 May 2019	Feather on train
10 May 2019	Picasso
23 May 2019	Maria's orbs
30 May 2019	The Montblanc Pen
20 June 2019	Gibberish in WhatsApp message box
21 June 2019	*Darling it's me* WhatsApp message on Maria's phone
22 June 2019	Feather aloft on jumper
22 June 2019	Raffle at French Night
1 July 2019	WhatsApp message
6 August 2019	WhatsApp groups
18 August 2019	Feather on train
20 August 2019	Feather in kitchen
31 October 2019	Maria's clock started to tick and a feather
9 November 2019	Rizla papers
8 January 2020	WhatsApp message
9 April 2020	WhatsApp messages
29 April 2020	WhatsApp messages
1 May 2020	New WhatsApp group
7 May 2020	Book flew off bookshelf
1 June 2020	WhatsApp message
12 September 2020	Book flew off bookshelf

7 October 2020	Playing card disappeared
29 October 2020	Ceiling lights came on
18 December 2020	Bookshelf lights came on
18 February 2021	Two new WhatsApp groups BulliesOut and newspaper report

References and Notes

Books mentioned

Schwartz, Dr Gary, *The Afterlife Experiments*, Atria Books, 2002
Kean, Leslie, *Surviving Death*, Three Rivers Press, 2017

Charity

BulliesOut
www.bulliesout.com
To contribute to the Patrick Hamlin Support Project, please visit
Louise Hamlin's justgiving page: www.justgiving.com

Podcasts

White Shores Season 3, episode 11. Theresa Cheung interviews
Louise Hamlin.

If you would like to share your experiences of grief or signs,
please visit www.louisehamlin.com

References and Notes

O-BOOKS

SPIRITUALITY

O is a symbol of the world, of oneness and unity; this eye represents knowledge and insight. We publish titles on general spirituality and living a spiritual life. We aim to inform and help you on your own journey in this life.

If you have enjoyed this book, why not tell other readers by posting a review on your preferred book site?

Recent bestsellers from O-Books are:

Heart of Tantric Sex
Diana Richardson
Revealing Eastern secrets of deep love and intimacy to Western couples.
Paperback: 978-1-90381-637-0 ebook: 978-1-84694-637-0

Crystal Prescriptions
The A-Z guide to over 1,200 symptoms and their healing crystals
Judy Hall
The first in the popular series of eight books, this handy little guide is packed as tight as a pill-bottle with crystal remedies for ailments.
Paperback: 978-1-90504-740-6 ebook: 978-1-84694-629-5

Take Me To Truth
Undoing the Ego
Nouk Sanchez, Tomas Vieira
The best-selling step-by-step book on shedding the Ego, using the teachings of *A Course In Miracles*.
Paperback: 978-1-84694-050-7 ebook: 978-1-84694-654-7

The 7 Myths about Love...Actually!
The Journey from your HEAD to the HEART of your SOUL
Mike George
Smashes all the myths about LOVE.
Paperback: 978-1-84694-288-4 ebook: 978-1-84694-682-0

The Holy Spirit's Interpretation of the New Testament
A Course in Understanding and Acceptance
Regina Dawn Akers
Following on from the strength of *A Course In Miracles*, NTI
teaches us how to experience the love and oneness of God.
Paperback: 978-1-84694-085-9 ebook: 978-1-78099-083-5

The Message of A Course In Miracles
A translation of the Text in plain language
Elizabeth A. Cronkhite
A translation of *A Course in Miracles* into plain, everyday
language for anyone seeking inner peace. The companion
volume, *Practicing A Course In Miracles*, offers practical lessons
and mentoring.
Paperback: 978-1-84694-319-5 ebook: 978-1-84694-642-4

Your Simple Path
Find Happiness in every step
Ian Tucker
A guide to helping us reconnect with what is really important in
our lives.
Paperback: 978-1-78279-349-6 ebook: 978-1-78279-348-9

365 Days of Wisdom
Daily Messages To Inspire You Through The Year
Dadi Janki
Daily messages which cool the mind, warm the heart and guide
you along your journey.
Paperback: 978-1-84694-863-3 ebook: 978-1-84694-864-0

Body of Wisdom
Women's Spiritual Power and How it Serves
Hilary Hart
Bringing together the dreams and experiences of women across
the world with today's most visionary spiritual teachers.
Paperback: 978-1-78099-696-7 ebook: 978-1-78099-695-0

Dying to Be Free
From Enforced Secrecy to Near Death to True Transformation
Hannah Robinson
After an unexpected accident and near-death experience, Hannah
Robinson found herself radically transforming her life, while a
remarkable new insight altered her relationship with her father, a
practising Catholic priest.
Paperback: 978-1-78535-254-6 ebook: 978-1-78535-255-3

The Ecology of the Soul
A Manual of Peace, Power and Personal Growth for Real People
in the Real World
Aidan Walker
Balance your own inner Ecology of the Soul to regain your
natural state of peace, power and wellbeing.
Paperback: 978-1-78279-850-7 ebook: 978-1-78279-849-1

Not I, Not other than I
The Life and Teachings of Russel Williams
Steve Taylor, Russel Williams
The miraculous life and inspiring teachings of one of the World's
greatest living Sages.
Paperback: 978-1-78279-729-6 ebook: 978-1-78279-728-9

On the Other Side of Love
A woman's unconventional journey towards wisdom
Muriel Maufroy
When life has lost all meaning, what do you do?
Paperback: 978-1-78535-281-2 ebook: 978-1-78535-282-9

Practicing A Course In Miracles
A translation of the Workbook in plain language, with
mentor's notes
Elizabeth A. Cronkhite
The practical second and third volumes of The Plain-Language
A Course In Miracles.
Paperback: 978-1-84694-403-1 ebook: 978-1-78099-072-9

Quantum Bliss
The Quantum Mechanics of Happiness, Abundance, and Health
George S. Mentz
Quantum Bliss is the breakthrough summary of success and
spirituality secrets that customers have been waiting for.
Paperback: 978-1-78535-203-4 ebook: 978-1-78535-204-1

The Upside Down Mountain
Mags MacKean
A must-read for anyone weary of chasing success and happiness
– one woman's inspirational journey swapping the uphill slog for
the downhill slope.
Paperback: 978-1-78535-171-6 ebook: 978-1-78535-172-3

Your Personal Tuning Fork
The Endocrine System
Deborah Bates
Discover your body's health secret, the endocrine system, and
'twang' your way to sustainable health!
Paperback: 978-1-84694-503-8 ebook: 978-1-78099-697-4

Readers of ebooks can buy or view any of these bestsellers by
clicking on the live link in the title. Most titles are published
in paperback and as an ebook. Paperbacks are available in
traditional bookshops. Both print and ebook formats are
available online.
Find more titles and sign up to our readers' newsletter at
http://www.johnhuntpublishing.com/mind-body-spirit
Follow us on Facebook at https://www.facebook.com/OBooks/
and Twitter at https://twitter.com/obooks